Rowing Tales

Rebecca Caroe

Rowing Tales

First Printing: November 2022

Dedication

You don't stop rowing because you get old. You get old because you stop rowing.

This volume is dedicated to all the masters rowers in the world. Keep on keeping on rowing.

From the Editor

I once thought that this volume of Rowing Tales would be a 'covid' edition. But I quickly found that there were no tales about rowing when rowers were training in isolation. What makes rowing such a special sport is our community, our meetings at regattas and camps and online - that's where our stories flow.

One of the most pleasurable parts of editing Rowing Tales is the sheer talent and diversity of experience that is brought forth by these short stories and anecdotes. It doesn't matter if you are not a rowing history buff - because the deep stories about rowing's past seem to surface themselves. It doesn't matter if you aren't on social media - because that's where the gentle teasing and online banter is shared. It doesn't matter if you no longer race - because racers are describing their experiences and we can vicariously live through their anecdotes.

Two of this year's stories relate to oft-written parts of rowing history that are hard to visualise. Firstly wooden boat building - who does it nowadays? We publish a detailed account of one person's attempt to build a racing shell out of wood when the expert practitioners are no longer around. And secondly, the Thames Waterman's rowing technique - much lauded as an efficient use of the water and physical endeavour to move a boat but only described in words - not pictures. I found a video in which Sherry Cassuto demonstrates how to row a waterman's catch in a modern single scull. The video link is included in her chapter.

US and British English spellings are used interchangeably, depending on the nationality of the author.

Thanks again go to the fabulous team who make this book possible - every author, I salute you. And also Gabrielle, Terri, Karlin and Laura - your professionalism is massively appreciated.

Rebecca Caroe
Auckland, New Zealand
October 2022

Authors

Henry Law & Andrew Isaac

Henry Law and Andrew Isaac enjoy rowing but sometimes feel the need to rail against the uninitiated whose murderous rowing machine technique serves as a cattle prod to watery rowers' sensibilities. They remember a time they got a different response.
On a discussion thread about erg technique in commercial gyms.

Mutual Recognition of Greatness

I used to travel a lot on business, so I had a list of company-approved hotels which had a fitness room with an erg in it, and I usually used it unless I had to work late.

One evening I sat down on one of two ergs (unusual), made my adjustments and started on a long low-intensity piece. I'd hardly started when a chap sat down on the other machine.

Oh, this is going to be fun, I thought. But when he set the drag factor properly I changed my view.

He warmed up a bit, then fell in with my low-ish rating. On and on we went, the dusk gathering outside, the sweat running, the noise of breathing starting to become more obvious until, after 10 km as I recall, I stopped. He stopped too. And we both sat for a moment, gathering our breath.

I stood up. He stood up. And put out his hand.

"Evesham Rowing Club," he said.
"Trafford Rowing Club," said I.

There was no need to say more.

Andrew Isaac replied:
Oh, East is East, and West is West, and never the twain shall meet.
Till Earth and Sky stand presently at God's great judgment seat.
But there is neither East nor West, border, nor breed, nor birth, when two strong men stand face to face, though they come from the ends of the earth!
Ready all, row.

Alan Clarence:
I was watching this guy once and he was really good.
Did a huge workout, and great technique. When he finished I complimented him and said he had a natural technique.
I introduced myself as a local club president and invited him to come and try in a boat.
He informed me he had done it before for a team I may have heard of called 'Australia'.

Cynthia de Joux:
Haha, I did that once.
Got invited to an open day. Went through the whole 'how to do it' intro, got in and rowed 500m behind my club member.
He stopped, turned around and said, ' You've done this before, haven't you?' I replied that I didn't want to appear as a know-it-all, but yes I have rowed for my country in my time.

Tonia Williams:

My tactic to diminish that feeling of 'self-anointed expert' when asked was to state simply "yes, I've done a bit of oaring."

Always worth the slight blush, creased brows, and then double-take to make sure they heard you right.

Niall Bates

Niall Bates is training for a very, very long row. The BCGE Tour du Léman à l'Aviron - a 160km rowing race around Lake Geneva done in coxed fours. He did a lot of preparatory training on the rowing machine.

Erg Heaven

I'm currently following the brutal but brilliant Eddie Fletcher rowing marathon plan (yet again) and today was a 90-minute session that I really, really didn't want to do.

So after spending the entire morning finding anything to do instead of my row, I finally trudged upstairs to the gym (that sounds dramatic, it's a spare room with an erg squeezed into it) like a condemned man on death row walking his final walk.

I sat down, looked at the program sheet and could not believe my eyes when I realised today was in fact *just* a 60-minute row and not a 90-minute one.

I don't think I've ever been as happy on an erg in my life.

It was the closest thing to an enjoyable 60 minutes on an erg that I can ever imagine doing.

Small wins.

John Frohnmayer

John Frohnmayer was an all-conference football player in high school, switched to golf at University and now, a lifetime later, he is a competitive rower with a drawer full of medals and the quixotic hope that his career as an athlete will never end.

John's trilogy of books on sports and philosophy, Socrates the Rower (courage, and self-knowledge); Carrying the Clubs (golf and ethics); and Skiing and the Poetry of Snow (glimpsing the world behind the world) are out there, inert, but steaming, waiting for you to pick them up, read them, and challenge your body and mind as you dive into life. His novel, Blood and Faith will be published November, 2022.

You will have heard of 12 step programs - they exist for many situations. While reading his Socrates the Rower book, I came across this passage. This is the first time I've seen a 12 Step Program for a 2K erg test.

12 Step Erg Test

After a periodic 2,000 meter test, one of our rowers wrote the twelve steps of rowing a 2K, which I reproduce here without adulteration or permission.

1. I admitted my legs are powerless - I am 1,200 meters into a 2K.
2. I have come to believe only a power greater than myself can get me through this piece.

3. Made a decision to turn my breathing over to God 'cause I sure as hell can't breathe on my own right now.
4. Made a searching and fearless moral inventory of my skill deficits.
5. Admitted to God, myself and another person that I was the one that crabbed in the high 15.
6. Was entirely ready to have God remove me from my seat.
7. Humbly pleaded with God to remove me from my seat.
8. Made a list of all persons I had harmed and became willing to make amends to them all.
9. Made a list of all of my possessions and decided who would get what, since I obviously am going to die.
10. Desperately begged God to remove me from my seat.
11. Seek through prayer and meditation an understanding of what heinous crime I had committed that this third 500 should be my penance.
12. Having had a spiritual awakening as a result of crossing the finish line, I tried to carry this message to other rowers.

Any similarity to the twelve steps of Alcoholics Anonymous is purely coincidental.

Charles Sweeney

Inspired by his daughter, Charles Sweeney returned to rowing after 25 years and now competes as a member of the Capital Rowing Club in Washington, DC, USA, balancing his training with a typical Washington career in politics and communications. He betrays his classical education with this reworking of a Roman Emperor's philosophic musings.

The Stoic As Oarsman

At dawn, when you have trouble getting out of bed, tell yourself;

"I have to go to [crew practice]. As a human being. What do I have to complain about, if I'm going to do what I was born for — the things I was brought into the world to do? Or is this what I was created for? To huddle under the blankets and stay warm?

So you were born to feel nice? Instead of doing things and experiencing them?

Don't you see the plants, the birds, the ants and spiders and bees going about their individual tasks, putting the world in order, as best they can?

And you're not willing to do your job as a human being? Why aren't you running to do what your nature demands?

You don't love yourself enough. Or you'd love your nature too, and what it demands of you."

-- *Marcus Aurelius*

Alan Clarence

Alan Clarence tells about how a guest row from a tourist led to one of the first para rowing races at the State Masters Championships. Leadership and vision in action.

Chance'd Be A Fine Thing

My association with Bairnsdale Rowing Club, Victoria, Australia, began some years ago. From a lazy 600 km away, Ivan contacted me and said "My wife and I are staying in Hamilton, could we have a social row with you guys?"

I replied "We are having a regatta, I have just entered you two in mixed doubles and you and I in masters doubles, so you had bet-ter turn up".

With a combined age of 128, there was no one comparable, so the local College put a couple of girls doubles against us and we won!

The cheeky commentator nicknamed us "Ivan from Bairnsdale and Ivan't won for 5 years." (Me being the latter!)

This began a friendship between Ivan and me and we have stayed in touch ever since.

In 2021, I was invited by Ivan and Bairnsdale RC to join in their men's masters quad at Footscray Regatta in Melbourne. We came 2nd narrowly beaten by Hawthorn, a big city club. Our training together consisted of two phone calls, three text messages and a row to the start line before the race.

8

Then, in 2022, at the Victorian State Championships, there was an event for para doubles where each crew had one or more para or special needs athletes. I had been rowing with a special needs friend from Nestle's (Warnambool) Club and Ivan said they had two guys at Bairnsdale who had special needs as well. So with a bit of organising, the three crews faced off at the State Champion-ships. After the race, we all got on the first-place winners podium together and gave each other three cheers. It made the local paper with the headline "Teamwork Makes The Dream Work".

To cap it off, the medal presenter, Alicia Ivory, who is a senior public servant, wrote to our captain about the experience of presenting to the para athletes.

"Over the weekend I had the privilege of awarding medals at the Victoria State Championships held by Rowing Victoria on Lake Wendouree in Ballarat.

The absolute highlight for me was awarding medals to these six men from Bairnsdale, Hamilton and Nestles rowing clubs who competed in the Para men's doubles. I have never seen such pas-sion, joy and good sportsmanship in any other event like it. Brought me to tears, and I'm so proud to be part of a sport that provides opportunities like these."

That chance connection with Ivan led to the most amazing and rewarding experience of my sporting life.

Irene Hewlett

This story comes from an exchange on social media. It started under a photo of four gentlemen around a green coxless four. The sun casts a shadow under the boat on its trestles and the crew are all grinning widely at the camera from under their caps. Little did I realise how far back this story went. The world of masters rowing is shrinking, seems everyone knows everyone else.

Friends For Life

Irene Hewlett took a little holiday diversion to a rowing club (who hasn't done that?).

While on holiday in Ireland we decided to pop by the rowing club where my husband attended a regatta about 30 years ago.

Just as we were there, three rowers appeared whose fourth quad member was unavailable so my husband jumped in as a sub and got to row for an outing!

If we'd have arrived five minutes earlier we would have left before meeting the local rowers and if we'd arrived five minutes later they would have gone out in singles. What amazing luck!!

Thank you St. Michael's Rowing Club (SMRC) Ireland for the hospitality!

Which prompted this rapid reply from Alan Clarence, a physical therapist in Adelaide, Australia.

I know the great story behind this photo which I hope you will enjoy...

A few years ago, I was emailed by a guy from a club 600 km away - asking if we would like a couple of extra rowers, he and his wife, to join my club training that upcoming weekend.

I replied that we had an informal regatta planned and had therefore entered them in a few events including us in a double so they had better turn up!

We won the men's masters doubles with the record oldest combined age (130+)!

And we have also since rowed together at state level, before COVID unfortunately prevented us competing at Nationals!

Friends ever since and even spoke today - Hamilton and Bairnsdale Rowing Clubs, Victoria, Australia.

All that just from one shared photo on Facebook.

Anja Wever

Anja Wever started a rowing "career" in Australia after a Learn to Row program, then joining an eight's crew and learning from the more experienced rowers. She passionately pursues all avenues to enhance her rowing technique.

Nepean Head First Timer

Nepean Head #1 – Single

The alarm went off at 4:45 am and it was bucketing down for my first Nepean time trial in a single.

I was feeling apprehensive; will I manage to row in a straight line? Will I manage to avoid the faster rowers? Will I be able to get the rigger onto the Lippy?

The drive down to the Nepean Rowing Club was in the lovely company of Joe and Beverley and we arrived to the hustle and bustle of many excited rowers. Despite the heavy rain, everybody was in good spirits. Our boats were already unloaded, and we started to rig.

My rigger went on without a hitch so I started walking the oars to the river nearby. Owen was at hand, helping walk the Lippy down the steep hill and helping me to get into the saddle. Beverley was already on the water waiting for me where she gave me a quick overview of the start and finish line.

We started rowing our way down to the 4km start line. The distance was reduced by 1,000m because of the currents. There was a massive wait as the rain continued, rain interspersed with the sounds of teeth chattering while thinking I would rather get back to my warm bed.

I started lining up and on the voice of "Number 75 go!" I took off and settled into a regular pace quite quickly. I managed to prevent a fellow competitor from overtaking me until the 3,000m line, avoided a green buoy..., and even managed to overtake another rower in my final sprint. I got to the finish line where enthusiastic supporters cheered us on.

There was Owen again, helping me out. Plus a lovely lady came from nowhere, offering a hand to carry my boat back up the steep hill to our trailer. Boat loading in the rain, more teeth chattering, and then a lovely breakfast organised by Beverley with our crew afterwards.

Reflecting on the day, I enjoyed every minute of it. I loved the enthusiasm of fellow rowers from other clubs, hearing their trials and tribulations and successes and the tremendous support of everybody.

I went home and had another story to tell. Took a snooze and managed to miss the boat unloading... and I came 5th – in my first single-time trial race.

Thanks, everybody!

Tania Lawlor

Tania Lawlor rows in Tralee, North Kerry, Ireland. She hails from France originally and took up rowing with the local club. Here she tells us about an unexpected ending to the club's time trial down the Ship Canal.

Low Tide Mud Bath

So yesterday with the Tralee Rowing club, we had our first time trial of the season. We had 15 people ready to participate in a range of crews - quad mixed quad, double, and single. We knew the tide was low, but that's not the first time we had raced at low tide.

When we arrived at the boathouse, we saw the tide was low, but the conditions were perfect, with no wind. So Jim decided to do 1,000 meters instead of 1,500 meters, just to be on the safe side.

We put the boats on the pontoon, and saw that the water was low, but we said that's okay. We will be careful steering coming back and the water will be a tiny bit lower in the next hour, but nothing that we can't deal with.

So we sent everyone up to the upper basin and everybody waited up there for the start. Everybody was happy.

We turned around so the single started first; two minutes later the double starts, then my coxed quad started and then two minutes later the coxless quad went.

We were happy with our row, we were careful and we are used to a narrow canal and were careful taking the corners and stuff.

We all did the 1,000 meter first race. After we all slowed down and started to row back to the pontoon. We were the first boat and we got stuck on a rock.

No one panics. We managed to unstick ourselves to move the boat around the rock and then we decided to slowly row back. We chose to row arms and body swing only and then just in case there were more rocks, we thought being in the middle of the canal would be better as the water is deeper there.

But there were rocks in the middle and so we stayed closer to the edge wall. Once we arrived close to the basin the double said to us "Stop there - there is no more water!"

But we still rowed on and we managed to row a bit closer and there was still a little bit of water under the boat. But then we tried to go around the final corner to go into the pontoon and then we got totally stuck.

The double managed to get to the pontoon and they waded out to help us. But for the two quads there wasn't enough water.

We were deep in the mud.

So everybody in all the boats stayed quite calm. And Jim was telling us what to do. He said to stay in the boat first and then the cox got out and one by one we got out of the boat. But by then the remaining water was totally gone. The tide went out very fast.

One by one we tried to push the boat to get it closer to the pontoon but since there was absolutely no water it was just pure mud and silt we couldn't move it. Jim threw us a safety rope and we attached it to both the boats, attaching it to one of the statues to anchor it.

Meanwhile we slowly tried to get out of the mud. But the mud came over my waist. Obviously, it's smelly and disgusting and it's a horrible feeling. We had to roll over doing some commando moves to get out of it. At one stage when I was starting to push the boats my ass got stuck under the weeds. It was really funny - NOT.

When we got closer to the canal side wall someone grabbed the oars and pulled me and we climbed up the wall and went back to safety. Everybody got out fine. All the silt came out of our clothes when we had a shower.

Strangely this had never happened before.

When we were back at the boathouse we decided to try to take the boats out of the mud but we changed our minds. And instead left the boats there to wait for the tide to come back in because we didn't want to damage them.

Just after the shower, Niamh decided to have a look and see if the lock gate was open because we were expecting to get a low tide but we had never seen the water go out that much before.

So we decided to go to have a look at the lock gate Unfortunately, the gate was open and that was what had drained all the water from the Canal. The water authority never told us, so the low water was something we could not have planned for. We were quite annoyed. Luckily we hadn't invited any other members of any other clubs to join the race.

So we had planned to go for a meal anyway - all the crew together - we went for a meal and came back to wait for the tide. And when we came back there was still no water!

We finally got the boats back in six hours later!

The boats were okay; they had a few scratches but no major damage and all the crew were safe. So that's one important thing. We were okay.

I forgot to say something. Walking into silt is not fun. But it was a good row and a good story too.

Jan Brosnahan

Jan Brosnahan started rowing before women really rowed, way back in 1976! Girls these days have no idea that "the old guys from that time would be surprised if they could see us women at the club now".

She lives in Dunedin, New Zealand and shares the delights of racing in the middle of winter (June) in the New Zealand south. The regatta has a number of humorously named trophies - some not awarded for rowing prowess.

South Island Masters Regatta In Dunedin

Queen's Birthday weekend saw the arrival in Dunedin of 220 masters rowers and supporters, mainly from the South Island but some from the North.

The South Island Masters Regatta has run for two decades and is always held on Queen's Birthday weekend. The first regatta was held at Port Chalmers but has enjoyed significant growth since then. The regatta rotates around the South Island clubs, with the last two regattas, planned by Ashburton/CURE, being cancelled due to the COVID pandemic in 2020 and the 2021 floods. Wakatipu held a successful regatta in 2019 on Lake Wakatipu and Lake Hayes.

Rowing in June, in Dunedin, is not for the faint-hearted and organisers were pleased with the excellent response. As many masters rowers coach over the summer and the calendar is full, this weekend is an opportunity to race and enjoy some social time over the long weekend.

We anticipated a frosty start, with associated calm water, and in fact, we enjoyed perfect rowing conditions. Saturday saw the long-distance race on the Taieri River, known as the Taieri–upon-Henley Bridge-to-Bridge, over 8.5 kilometres. That's 8.5 kilometres to the start and a race of 8.5 kilometres back, again, not for the pusillanimous. Chosen for the scenery, the quiet water and surrounds, plus the proximity to Lake Waihola, it is described as one of the best rowing routes in New Zealand.

A bonus was the ability to beach boats at the Taieri Mouth end, before the race proper. Onlookers at the Taieri Mouth Bridge enjoyed a spectacle as the sun glistened on the water and the many crews in different club colours wove their way down the river.

The strategy of taking the shortest distance was challenged along the twisting river, however, the scenic course offered a novelty for rowers. With 32 crews entered in a variety of boats and leaving at one-minute intervals, crews jostled to contest some coveted trophies including the "Mock Rooster" and "Port Parrot."

The crack Picton crew finished fastest in 32 minutes 44 seconds, taking home the Bluebridge Trophy. Dan Karena, along with three Gaudin brothers – Keiran, Ryan and Hayden – took the race by the scruff of the neck, putting time into the favoured eights.

Picton carried this through to Sunday where they were winners of A and B single and double sculls, B pair, B 4- and 4x and combined in the 8+. Their enthusiasm has extended to volunteering to host the 2023 event. The winner of the Port Parrot for fastest women's quad was North End.

In a nod to the Coast-to-Coast, all competitors finishing the long-distance race were given a can of Emerson's product.

The Sunday racing over 1,000 metres on Lake Waihola was generally very close. Several trophies for overall honours were at stake, meaning handicaps needed to be applied to all events in each class throughout the day to negate the ageing effect – i.e. results of A-D races had to be matched against E-I races and handicaps applied to reveal the eventual "fastest" winner. This also ensured crews didn't ease up and it was effectively a "sealed handicap."

Starting with mixed races at 9 am, the fixtures moved to five-year age group events and finished with the feature eights at 3 pm. With many race classes available, there was a fair bit of boat-hopping and some quick turnarounds. The women's eight was won by North End/Invercargill and the men's eight won by Wakatipu/North End.

Dave Hanan, North End, was again awarded "Stew's Stirrer". Dave towed the club boats from the closest club but still managed to arrive just in the nick of time. However, on arrival, he realised he had left oars at home, but thought he could make the 1.5-hour round trip in less than half an hour.

The Mercer Trophy, for the club with the largest number of wins, was awarded to the Avon Club. The Terry Noonan Trophy for the rower or official showing commitment to rowing was awarded to Deb Hymers-Ross, Union, by previous recipient Maude O'Connell, Cromwell.

Oldest competitors were local legends Faye Forgie and Lorna Bain (both 76), Port Chalmers United, and John Wilson, (77), Riverton. Lorna is a novice and teamed up with Ross Johnston (76 and also a novice). Rowing is a challenging sport to take up as we age, so kudos to these very courageous Port Chalmers rowers.

The weekend incorporated two social events; a barbeque along with Emerson's product post-long distance; and a dining and dance event on Sunday evening. Monday was a well-deserved rest day.

For many competitors, the weekend was nostalgic as they re-lived racing on Lake Waihola in the seventies and eighties, before the creation of Lake Ruataniwha.

As many commented, racing at Waihola is hit-and-miss as the lake is exposed to the southerly. How lucky we were.

Elliza McGrand

Elliza McGrand shares how she learns to race hard and the new challenges which guide her progress though racing single sculls.

Gail Pushing My Boundaries

This weekend I raced a single in California as part of my preparation for the upcoming Head of the Charles races (HOCR). I picked this regatta because I would race a group of the fastest rowers from the west coast who go to the HOCR.

I came in 5 of 7. It confirmed something I already pretty much knew - it's unrealistic to expect to win this race. It also confirmed something I was hoping - I was in the pack, with a time not horribly below people who are winning there.

I have real hope that my first single race at the HOCR (and you only get one, first time single HOCR race in your life) might go ok, although the course and steering in Boston are much harder. And if my single race goes ok, my double race is even more likely to be ok too.

It isn't an ego boost to go to a tough race you're unlikely to win, but I think it's how you learn and get better. And I, and the scullers know, think if you show up and race your single, then do it again after that, you've already won wherever you place in the finish order.

It is terrifying and lonely and feels very exposed, but I have real hope racing my single will eventually be more joyful than anything else.

This weekend, on the funky, sunny, often beautiful Head of the Port course in Sacramento, while rowing a gorgeous Sykes single I had moments of joy in my beautiful boat, in this beautiful place, with these extraordinary women!

One woman, Gail Brownell, rowed alongside me and fought me every meter of the course. I never took a meter she didn't take back, and she never stopped coming for me.

It was one of the most extraordinary races (and gifts) from a rower of my life. She beat me on handicap and she earned that win in blood. She was amazing.

May I be Gail in my racing.

Roger Milne

Roger Milne recalls his very first World Rowing regatta as an umpire. He had a challenging time at the first Rowing World Cup during 2010. Roger says he's not a superstitious man, but he did think that the "Gods of Lake Luzern" were out to get him that weekend.

The Race Umpire follows each race in a speed boat. The Start umpire stands behind the start and prepares the crews, reads the crew lane order 'roll call' and starts the race.

The rules of racing were changed after this regatta so that any dead heats in semi finals no longer require a re-row because it disadvantages those crews relative to the rest of the competitors.

Muggins is a British English expression of self-deprecating humour.

The Hauraki Gulf and islands are popular boating waters near Auckland, New Zealand.

Why Me, God?

On the first morning of racing I was Judge at the start – at the exact same time as the starter's horn sounded, a kid slid down the slope behind me and whacked the back of the corrugated iron-clad shed I was standing inside and I nearly had kittens!

Late morning one – I was moved to being the race starter. It was the heat of the women's eight and the weather had turned to very hot conditions.

I led the roll call, pressed the start button; nothing happened. Russia was racing in lane 2, so I guessed it was no use saying anything as they are unlikely to understand English. So with confident advice from my Swiss colleague standing alongside that the system wouldn't malfunction twice, I simply started the roll call again, and pressed the start button, with the same silent result – so I said "GO", and away they went, without fuss! (or any timing). So much for "Swiss timing reliability"!

Later, there had been a serious storm overnight, which saw trees downed and the suspended numbers above the start were wound around the overhead wires. Fortunately, there was no damage in the boat park.

Come Saturday afternoon I was back as race umpire of the men's quadruple sculls semi final.

I delivered a normal start, the driver in my umpire launch steered me in behind the crews, and I noticed a boat coming towards us from the other end of the lake. There was nothing unusual about that because after each race, the race umpire's launch has to return to the start to officiate another race. Normally boats drive down the centre of the lake and then pull to the side to allow a race to pass.

Italy were in lane 5 and New Zealand in lane 6. The race progresses to around 1,100 metres, when I heard a very Swiss German voice crackle over the radio. My boat driver translated what she'd heard "you must stop zee race".

I asked her to verify that this is correct, as I couldn't see any reason to stop a race in the 3rd quarter. By this time we were approaching 1,400 meters gone ....more radio chatter........"you must stop zee race!".

So up goes my red flag and dingle dingle goes the bell. Effective stopping of the race immediately.

I can now see the reason.

The TV camera boat had got its propeller firmly attached to the lane buoy line between lanes 4 and 5. As it was steering to the side of the lake it was dragging the buoys so that Italy had an ever-decreasing lane width.

While we guide the Italian crew to change direction to avoid colliding with the TV boat, Matt Trott in the bow of the Kiwi quad looks over his shoulder, recognises me and realises I am the umpire and with a big, loud (across water) voice, says "This wouldn't happen at Karapiro eh Rog!"

With the "who's who" of World Umpiring watching on closely, I really did think my umpiring days were over!

By Sunday morning my duties had moved to being the responsible Judge at the Finish. It was the semifinal of the men's coxless pair. The Republic of South Africa win. But I had a different problem - Germany in lane 6 and Australia in lane 1 have dead heated.

Because it's a semi-final, only 2 crews can progress to the final. So a row-off is required. Muggins signs it off, much to the displeasure of the Australian Team Manager, who made his feelings known at the door of the judges' room. I was very thankful for support from the Chair of the World Rowing Umpires Commission who happened to be sitting beside me!

By the end of the regatta on Sunday night I sought to have a quiet discussion with the President of the Jury, as to why all this has happened to me in my very first outing as a World Rowing Umpire.

"Don't worry" he says – "all is good. Hey, by the way, I'm coming to New Zealand later in the year for the World Rowing Championships. I'm also a sailing coach, and I'd love to charter a yacht and go for a sail – any ideas?"

We had friends with a 65 foot yacht on a mooring in Maharangi. "No need to charter" says I "we'll sort something." Fast-forward to the week after the Worlds at Karapiro 2010. Sailing with said Swiss friend across the Hauraki Gulf after a couple of splendid nights at Great Barrier Island.

The Swiss umpire was on the helm, the owner had his head in a locker, me in the galley making coffee. He sails into a huge school of kahawai fish, complete with gannets and dolphins! All four of us were enjoying coffee and the spectacle before us, when, as if we had dialled them up, half a dozen orca whales came along for a look!

One of those unforgettable moments, a long way from Luzern!

Chris Brake

Chris Brake is a coach and rower from Blenheim, New Zealand. He is a 'hard man' of the sport, having been known to enter eight separate events in a single one day 1k regatta... and medal in seven of them.

The Maadi Cup is the New Zealand Secondary Schools Regatta and this trophy is awarded to the Under 18 schoolboy eights event. The cup was brought to New Zealand by returning Second World War Veterans who did a boat race in Maadi outside Cairo, Egypt after being demobilised and waiting for ships to take them home.

2083

One of my coaching colleagues was resetting the numeric padlock on our boat trailer box and said he'd picked the number 2083.

We asked why?

He said because the last time the local High School won the the Maadi cup was 1983 and it'll be a hundred years before they do so again!

Makes me laugh every time I open the padlock.

Cam Brown

Cam Brown is an Australian working as the Head Coach at Orange County College in California, USA. In this tale he talks about the challenges of coaching collegeiate rowing and the linguistic challenges when his American students cannot understand his Aussie slang.

Watch the full interview: https://youtu.be/2c9eOX-ReJg

Word Games on the Erg

I thought about this a few years ago. When we're doing a long steady state row on the water or trying to mix up a steady state session on the erg and I thought we needed ways to break up the long session and make it a little more lighthearted.

Sometimes I will be briefing the crews and all of a sudden I see all these blank faces staring back at me. I will have used some term or some word that they have no idea what I'm talking about.

And so I realised they need to understand Australian phraseology much better. So on a trip back to Australia, I stopped by the airport, and grabbed one of these books, the Great Australian Slang Book.

It's got all the different letters of the alphabet, and the Australian definitions of certain terms.

During a long erg I'll get the athletes to pick out a letter, and then we'll get to see what the book says. It helps teach them how to speak Australian a little bit. Some are in better taste than others.

Give us some examples.

The letter R. So here are three "definitions" from the letter R.

As rare as rocking horse shit. You know this is very uncommon.

Ready as a drover's dog. I'll let you guess the meaning. But someone out on the town on a Saturday night might be as ready as that!

Ready to drop. When someone is pregnant.

But it's a bit of fun to kind of break up the monotony of training and teach the guys a little bit of Aussie culture at the same time.

Katie Zaferes

Katie Zaferes is a triathlete. I heard her speak at the Outspoken Women Triathletes event. This poem is an inspiration for me and I hope for you too.

Breathe For Your Racing Mind

Breathe in adaptability, breathe out concern,
No matter what happens there's something to learn.

Breathe in strength, breathe out weakness,
Now is the time to let go of your meekness.

Breathe in bravery, breathe out comfort,
Risk often leads to being triumphant.

Breathe in resilience, breathe out pain,
Everyone's hurting but your strength will remain.

Breathe in self focus, breathe out distraction,
Do not let comparison lead to detraction.

Breathe in community, breathe out isolation,
This whole journey has been a collaboration.

All you breathe in encompasses you,
Ready to conquer what you came to pursue.

Charles Wemyss

Charles Wemyss started rowing by chance, having met and watched a sculler during his summer vacations in New England at Mirror Lake and Lake Placid, New York. This encounter started a lifetime's involvement in the sport. He was a member of Union Boat Club which he describes as 625 men who played squash and 25 who rowed!

He is an accomplished masters athlete and high school coach.

Quit Bugging Me!

I was this little kid and this old fellow kept a beautiful old single at the lake. And each day I'd help him wet launch and then wipe the boat down after the outing. And I would say "Mr .... Please teach me to row". And he'd say "No. I have six children and I said no to all of them and it's no to you too".

The next summer when I was 15 I did it again.

And on the very last day of the season when we were taking the boat out of the water for the last time, without any real warning he said, "get in."

And I sat in the boat.

The oars were all the same size In those days and my hands couldn't go around the handles. So I just hooked on and he explained what I should do. He was holding the stern of the boat as I started to row...

He said "Take a big stroke - can you let the boat go?"

And I went shooting across the lake. I felt this instant transition. And so I yelled out "Hey, what do I do now?" and he replied "You row!"

And I've never forgotten that. It made so much sense.

Even though I rowed poorly initially, letting the boat go just made sense to me.

The man was Peter Kiernan, and it was at Mirror Lake and Lake Placid, upstate New York. Peter created what is now Bank of America. He gave me this wonderful thing - rowing.

I can remember the day it all started. I still actually have funny little photographs that he took of me.

He was sitting down and watching me rowing. He had this old stupid camera and he took these photographs. And I found them at my Mother's house. I thought "Holy crap, look at these - this is from 1971!"

There were two things that would happen to me while I was coaching or rowing when I always think of Pete, and the gift that he gave me. This wonderful thing that changed everything in my life. I still get verklempt about it.

It made me survive officer candidate school in the Marine Corps. It made me survive bad days as an infantry officer in the Marine Corps. It's that esprit de corps.

When I coached, I would tell our athletes, when you come down that hill you come into my little world, you leave everything behind. Fight with the teacher, fight with the girlfriend, fight with the boyfriend, flat tires, everything. That stops at the edge of the road here. And for the next 90 minutes all we're going to worry about is this. And then when you go back to the world, you're going to be a lot better off because you'll have just left it all behind and you'll have to concentrate on this very counterintuitive, physically difficult sport and make it work.

And the point is, when you get that kind of event in your life, and it comes from rowing it's game changing. You know, it's why I won't quit,

I've always thought it would be good to tell this story and to send it to Peter Kiernan's family. Do you guys know what your Dad did? You know, your Dad is a fabulous man. I would see him when I was home during the holidays, he knew I was rowing in college, and he would say "And just remember, you know, just remember who got you started!"

I'd be out coaching and I'd be losing my mind. And I would look up and I would say to myself, "What would you do, Pete? You know, help me, what do I do?"

Of course he never answered but the answer was self-evident because he coached me enough so I knew.

Telling this tale would be a better way to do it than sending a letter - put it in a book. Right?

Jim Dietz

Jim Dietz has been racing in a single for many years - he has rowed every Head of the Charles since 1965 when the first race was held.

He told me this story while describing how to steer the Head of the Charles, turn by turn.

Watch the full interview https://www.youtube.com/watch?v=3loRpTdjwYQ

The Seth Thomas Clock Company started making timepieces in 1813.

Synchronized Timing Systems

So back in the day at the very first head of the Charles the starting line was comprised of state of the art equipment.

There was a Seth Thomas clock like you'd see in a classroom, you know about ten inches round with a second hand on it mounted onto a piece of three quarter inch plywood.

As you rowed by, with a state of the art Polaroid camera, they would take a picture of you.

And later, as you crossed the line at the finish, there was another clock with another Polaroid camera, supposedly synced up with the one at the start, where they took a second picture of you.

Those pictures were then sent to the Cambridge Boat Club where they did the math to figure out the finishing order.

And that's why the beer party at the Harvard cage lasts till about three o'clock in the morning!

There was a lot of math in the old days.

David Hickey

David Hickey spent lockdown writing his rowing autobiography - he was a youthful scamp at Trinity College Dublin in the 1970s where he was first introduced to rowing. It's called The Trinity College VIII.

Subsequently, he did a number of Masters events for Old Collegians and Tideway Scullers School in Munich, Viareggio, and various locations in Holland. You can occasionally see him out with Scullers and Walbrook, both on different stretches of the Thames in London.

Rowing Made Them

It is often repeated that sport is a microcosm of society. If sport is defined by darts, synchronised swimming and dressage, then I really do fear for society. If on the other hand, sport can be defined as rowing, then we are in a very safe place. The reason I say this is as follows.

Many years back, as a voluntary rowing coach, I was helping out Tony Brook (highly successful New Zealand rower in the late 1970s/early 1980s) who was Head of Rowing at Kings College School, Wimbledon, UK. At the time, the small school rowing squad rented a few bays from another club on the upper Kingston reach of the Thames.

One day, Tony approached me to say that there was a boathouse at Putney (further down river, and in many ways the home of London rowing), which was being sold. He wanted the school to buy it. The fact that the Cambridge crews used it for the annual Varsity boat race (and still do) would, he thought, assist in convincing the school. Fearing that the school might not have the requisite finances available however, he asked me to assist in raising funds. I suggested however that the first priority would be to secure permission from the school for the venture. He agreed, spoke to the headmaster and a meeting of the school governors was quickly convened to hear the case.

And so at 7pm one midweek evening, the dozen or so governors assembled. A significant number of interested parents also showed up, as did many of the teachers. All in all, there was quite a crowd. Tony was first up and made the rowing case. I followed extolling the financial virtues of riverside property in London, and finally the headmaster made the point that a central London footprint for the school would immeasurably enhance its status. As I watched the reaction, it became abundantly obvious to me that the governors were completely unpersuaded, and were clearly wondering how quickly they could decently escape from this drivel, and settle down for the evening in the nearby pub. That's when the chairman of the board noticed that we also had with us, the headmaster of the Junior School.

Now a good chairman in any walk of life doesn't simply listen to those banging on at the meeting. They will also be keeping an eye out for those who remain silent. Of course, folk can be quiet for two reasons. Firstly they can follow the sound advice which my late mother used constantly to hand out to me, which was "better to keep your mouth shut and be thought a fool, than open it and remove all doubt". The other reason for silence however is that the individual is thinking carefully and is probably worth hearing.

This chairman realised that in Colin Holloway, the Junior School had a leader who was well known for his perspicacity in analysing growing boys. Whether from a social, familial, physical, emotional, or dry educational viewpoint, Colin was extraordinarily gifted in being able to assess the young charges passing through his school. But whatever his existing reputation, what he proceeded to say in the room that evening quite floored everyone.

Each year, he said, some 40 to 50 boys leave my school and progress to the senior school. Of those, there are usually 3 to 5 who, I conclude sadly, will not make it in society. Occasionally however, one of those boys will join the rowing club. I have seen this happen about a dozen times in the years I have been here. In every single such case, the boy concerned has changed beyond belief, and by the time they depart the senior school, it has given me the greatest of pleasure to have to reverse completely my previous opinion of that lad. Whatever you do in rowing, he said, it seriously benefits these boys and everyone with whom they will come into contact.

He concluded by saying very quietly, if buying this boathouse increases the likelihood of more such boys benefitting, then it is not just that I would favour the purchase, I would regard it as the civic duty of all of us to support the proposal.

Needless to say there followed a stunned silence. The chairman didn't even look around him for soundings. He looked straight at Tony Brook and said, you have the full support of this committee. Please come to me at any time for any further support required.

KCS has owned that boathouse ever since.

Dwight Jacobson

Dwight Jacobson grew up in NY, and first started rowing at Marist College in Poughkeepsie NY where he stroked the lightweight 8. Later he began sculling with a Martin Trainer, which he hauled up to Alaska and rowed on remote lakes. After Alaska, he settled in Seattle where he's been a member of The Pocock Rowing Center and Lake Washington's Rowing Club.

Seattle is the site of the "Ship Canal", the waterway that links the Puget Sound with Seattle's Lake Union where the club boat houses are located.

He's humbler than he used to be about single sculling.

Rowing In Fog

I was rowing down what we call around these parts, the "ship canal", certain there wasn't another soul alive that would be dumb enough to be out in such conditions, mostly feeling glib that I had the whole universe to myself.

Usually, I'd check for traffic every ten strokes or so, but because I was sure I was alone, I decided to save the wear and tear on my neck for who knows, maybe forever.

Finally, I decided to turn around.

At that moment, there was a big tug boat, crawling up the canal. I saw the skipper in the wheelhouse on his cell phone, cool as a cucumber, seemingly also sure there were no other fools out.

He saw me at precisely the same moment I saw him.

I lifted the oars in a panic stop, and he threw the tug in a full-power reverse.

The whole Zen experience of being in my "dream" came to a heart-pounding stop. I woke up, humbled, and electrified.

I rowed home with my tail between my legs, glad I didn't crash my shell and go for a swim.

Kelley Kassa

Kelley Kassa replied to Facebook to a beautiful image taken by Blair Granum of Lake Quinsig, Central Massachusetts, USA.

She lives in Boston, MA, USA and learned to row 22 years ago at CRI. Mostly she rows recreationally, and started coaching at CRI in 2022, coaching middle schoolers, adults, and young adults with intellectual disabilities.

Ghostly Craft

I have a great story about rowing on Lake Quinsig.

I got a seat in one of their 8+s for the Head of the Charles Regatta. Unlike at my regular club, Community Rowing Inc (a club in Boston, MA), the rowers don't learn to cox. So I offered to cox Friday morning practices, while rowing for the other practices.

My first or second time coxing… it's 5ish am, dark & foggy. I'm approaching the bridge.

Suddenly I see a moored sailboat appearing in the fog. Straight in front of me.

I managed to avoid it (without stopping)!

Once we get past it the stroke tells me, "Oops. We forgot to tell you to take the middle arch."

Blair Granum replied: Wait… So you went far right?!

Kelley replied: Yup. I was very calm about almost hitting the sail boat. I had enough time to just clear it. The darn thing was like Brigadoon - appeared out of nowhere.

Sean Colgan

Rowing coaches are a breed apart. Some are utterly unique. Sean Colgan spent his lockdown profitably compiling anecdotes from the oarsmen who had been coached by Ted A. Nash.

His published the "Book Of Ted" which hit the shelves in fall 2022. Get a copy for yourself.

He kindly allowed me to reproduce a few of the stories here.

Ted A. Nash

Daylight, a Saturday AM row. Connelly Container Twin Stones location, spinning the frosh eight, getting ready for a long continuous pull down to the Viking. We were just starting the piece when I felt a sting. A teenage punk on the east bluff of the Schuylkill River had a high-powered pellet gun and was using us as target practice.

Louie Wolfe the cox calls Ted over, as blood is on my shirt. I'm shot on the underside of my left bicep. Ted takes one look and says, Can you row? Sure... He wheels his boat around, beaches into the urban rubble lining the steep bank, and sprint-clambers up the Manayunk detritus.

As Ted is climbing, he glances up to see the sunlight glinting off the rifle barrel. He raises his hand, and a pellet shoots right through it. Ted grabs

the rifle, breaks it over his knee, drags the kid into the launch, and binds his hands with duct tape so he can finish coaching. Afterward, he deposited the kid at the Community boathouse, where the river police had a station.

At the arraignment, instead of juvenile detention in a lockup, Ted requested that this JD be released into his "care" for several weeks— community service at the boathouse! Ted wanted to teach him respect for oarsmen!

Hugh Stevenson, Penn '72, Olympics '76

In 2004, the men's eight final training for the Athens Olympics was in Plovdiv, Bulgaria. The fin was a very special one, as we had trialed a few different options. Finally the EXACT right custom-made fin was selected.

On the race course at Plovdiv, there was a cable that ran under the water holding the lane buoys. At the end of a piece, we heard the fin go. Pete checked and confirmed it was gone—and alerted Mike, who was on his bike. When he realized the fin was gone, he was not happy. Ted was biking behind Mike. When he realized what was happening, he ghosted his bike, sprinted to the water, and dove in. Ted disappeared under the water—and a few seconds later he popped up, holding the fin in his teeth.

Our eight went on to win the gold medal in Athens.

Dan Beery, Olympics '04

Ted executed a perfect dive into the lake, surfacing moments later with the skeg in his teeth. Amazing! I have never met anyone else whose "Gives-a-Shit Meter" was so consistently pegged at 11.

Matthew Deakin, Olympics '04

Whenever I see someone carrying four carbon fiber oars down to the dock, I ask if they've ever heard of Ted Nash. They usually say, "I've heard of him, but I never met him."

I respond, "Ted used to carry eight wooden sweep oars in one trip!"

John Everett, MIT '75, Olympics '76, '80

A warm spring day, in the middle of a two-mile piece on the Schuylkill, passing the Canoe Club.

Joe O'Conner, the cox of one eight, says: "Coach, there is a dead body floating just off my starboard bow."

Ted: "Keep rowing, son. The guy will be there when we come back down the river."

And he was...

Sean Colgan, Penn '77

Ted Nash taught you to do things that you did not know you could do. Ted Nash taught you not to set limits on what you could achieve. Ted Nash freed you to see how good you could be. He taught you the process by which you achieve excellence. Although Ted taught this in rowing, the process is transferable and is applicable to other aspects of one's life. He was simply the most extraordinary person I have ever had the privilege to meet, and he changed my life dramatically for the better. At Ted's surprise eightieth birthday party, what struck me most was that each and every person in that room had had the trajectory of their lives changed by Ted Nash. That is a remarkable legacy.

Tim Thompson, Penn '72

I was fortunate enough to be a member of the 1968 Penn Freshman crew that went undefeated and unheaded. Never lost and no crew was ever ahead of us.

In our first Ted lecture on our first day at the boathouse, he told us that Harvard was our toughest competition. We had a bus that transported us from the campus to the boathouse and back, and Ted instructed us: "When you come off the bus every day, you RUN through the front door and yell BEAT HARVARD! as loudly as you can!"

Our first race against Harvard was to be in the Adams Cup in Annapolis in April. A few weeks before the race, we had the following workout: "Take the boat to the top and warm up. We are doing just ONE 500-meter piece today." Confused over such a light workout, we did as we were told.

We turned around at the top and Ted advised: "Let the boat drift down to the start line. When you hit it, I will say, 'GO!,' and I want you at 50 strokes a minute for the entire piece."

500 meters at 50 seemed impossible, but Ted had spoken. To this day, more than fifty years later, I can remember how wound up we were!

As we approached the 1000-meter mark: "Get ready... get ready... GO!"

We are all convinced these many years later that the boat leapt out of the water! We launched at 52 strokes per minute. Ted had the big megaphone, and his voice across the water was like the voice of God. "REACH! STAY LONG! KEEP THE RATE UP!"

He paused then. No sound but 8 oars pounding the water at 50.

Then..."When you get to the 500, DON'T STOP! TAKE IT TO THE FINISH LINE!"

Impossible! But Ted had spoken. We did (of course) and at the end of it I was sure I was going to die—we all were. 1000 meters at 50? Impossible...

Fast forward to the Adams Cup race. We were quick off the line for the lead. Then Harvard started to creep back. From the 1500 to the 1000, Harvard came to within a seat. I was stroking and our coxswain, Terry Regan, glared at me and said, "We gotta go... NOW!"

And we did... rate went to 40, then 42, then 44. Harvard tried to stay with us, but they had never done 1000 meters at 50. We had.

Ted allowed us to find a place during those 500 meters at 50 that turned into 1000 meters we never would have found alone. He showed us that the limits we place on ourselves can be exceeded.

Over the years I would often summon that feeling when presented with a tough business situation. "This looks really hard...but not as hard as 1000 meters at 50! Let's get busy!"

Rick Crooker, Penn '71

I remember it all like it was yesterday. We lost two races in a row my freshman year: the first was Class Day and then Princeton. Immediately after that race, Ted took over coaching us. Steve Orova was relegated to the second frosh.

The rest is history, as Gary coxed us to an undefeated remainder of the season.

Ted's pre-race talks were spot-on and legendary. He always painted a realistic picture of what to expect. Before one race, he told us our opponents had a tremendous start and we could be down two lengths after 500 meters— which we were—and that we would walk through our opponents in the middle 1000—which we did. As we passed the 500-meter mark, Gary shouted into the microphone, "We are at 500 meters two lengths down, right where we want to be!" I will never forget that.

John Cartus, Penn '78

In 2014, thirty-seven years after I had last rowed for the Quakers, I awoke in an ICU bed after a seven-hour heart surgery. I was nervous and scared and in considerable pain. The room was full of flowers, which, my wife explained, had been sent by Penn rowing alums. The silence in the room was broken by the ring of my cell phone. When my wife answered, I heard, "This is Coach Nash" on the other end, and disoriented as I was, whatever anesthesia I was under quickly wore off. "Son," Ted said to me, "you have faced tougher obstacles and I taught you to be tough. Your Penn Brothers are pulling for you and you will recover."

I will never forget that day. After all those years, Ted still checked on one of his athletes at a difficult time. The years at Penn rowing for Ted gave me the discipline to succeed in my career, but it took one phone call to understand the measure of the man. He was more than a coach; he was a mentor and friend, and he never forgot his oarsmen.

Rowing masters, I would see Ted at various regattas. My club team was very impressed that I had rowed for the "legend" Ted Nash. I once asked him to speak to my teammates at Masters Nationals, and he spoke to a captive audience for thirty minutes about the sport of rowing and the value of "brotherhood."

Ted's success on the water is only part of the story. He had a human side, a caring side, and he knew his words had an effect on people. I was one of the lucky ones who knew Ted on the water and off... and I will be forever grateful.

Bob Johnson, Penn '78

Elliza McGrand

Elliza McGrand tells about a reckless yet beautiful outing she did in her single scull.

Debris Danger

Our river was glass yesterday morning. It's getting late in the season so my club won't go out anymore except on weekends, when the sun is up. I've been going out for the last few weeks around 5:30-6ish. This week of post-Charles breathing and loosening, so far I've gone out once at 06:38 and yesterday at 06:26. I'm aiming to be out by 05:55/06:00 again. But it's... scary. Insanely beautiful and scary.

The sky is black with swirls and connect-the-dot stars. It's cold, and except for the occasional insomniac reading and drinking coffee in their living room, I'm completely alone. No one will go out in the dark except (occasionally) my 2x partner in a double with me. And it's cold.

There's not much ambient light near the dock at the launch point. Once off the dock I cross the river into a line of buoys that demarcate the open river from the floating house frontage. There's no lights or reflecting tape on the buoys and they're irregularly placed. I've hit one (and near missed) a buoy more than once. They can be boat tippers. Once the buoys are behind me, I dodge the rocks and remnants of an old dock; the whirlpool before the bridge; then through the bridge arch, wet stone stretching up the sides.

Past the bridge, the Willamette river widens into what has been nicknamed "Thunderdome." This is a 3,000 meter stretch of river with floating houses and a boatyard along one side, and woods and shore along the other. On weekends and afternoons motorboats and jet skis zoom up and down, throwing wakes at kayaks and sculls and stand-up paddleboarders.

Up to now it's been survival/steering rowing with a splash of warm-up. Lately I've begun forcing myself to stop past the bridge and do a chop drill - alone in the dark and the cold and my fear. I shake, my legs shake, but I force myself to do it and remember, find, the iron cage of balance - pressure of oars against oarlocks, length of blade. After what some mornings seems like a universe of time, it will click in and I'll stop quaking and unbalancing with my legs.

Then I really row. I stretch past the big (perhaps abandoned) ferry, past the sailing club, the elaborate houses, the "castle". I'm warming, shedding gear, finding rhythm. I get to maybe the bay, maybe just past it, then I have to turn around.

At some point before the bay I get ambitious. I start with the 10s, the absolute focus on technical steps, boatfeel. Then, feeling as if I'm cheating myself - while my Van Dusen is giving me slightly nagging reminders of the time in chilly New England dialect - I turn. Then I start stretching it out again, passing steering beacons and shibboleths like a snagged tree, the country club dock.

I go to fast mode, row-hard mode. I realize I'm late. I go into a straight-up fast piece rate. And I hit the debris field that inevitably lurks right in front of the boatyard. It makes me nervous. I have a track record of 'encounters' with the debris field.

48

In the past, I've completely lost hold of an oar and watched it jump in front of me like a gun running away from a gunslinger. My boat has hit a fireplace-sized log with a clunk, my oar slammed into a bottle somehow without breaking it. I've screamed my way past suicidal geese perched on submerged logs.

But today I make it safely to the Sellwood bridge and shoot through an arch. I want to claim that sacred rest zone past the bridge, but I've inevitably dawdled, I'm late, and the world is slapping at me. I dock in the beginnings of light, practically run with the boat and oars to the boathouse. And I don't want to. I want to row longer, to linger on the dock taking pictures and checking my distance and heart rate on my phone.

As I drive in to work, the sun is rising, the river is glass, and fleets of kayaks in crayon colors are out.

It's terrifying, beautiful, a gift I tear out of my club's disapproval and the (honestly) stupidity of this act. But it's the only chance I have to be on the water. I'm beautifully alone - no negotiation, free to go ahead and be reckless, glide under the stars in the cold and wind and chop.

Henry Law

Henry Law rows with Trafford Rowing Club in Manchester, Great Britain and is an active contributor to online rowing discussions. This time he started something which maybe was more than he expected would be the case. Sometimes it pays to be provocative just to be 'ornery. The discussion was lengthy and heated.

Henry's Knack For Starting Discussions

Let's see if there's a discussion to be had...

My thesis; from the point of view of a non-rower spectator, rowing races are dull as ditch water!

Let's start with the most engaging format, the head-to-head match race. You're standing at halfway, the commentary says the race has started, and after a bit, two crews heave into view. You can't tell which is which, nor (because of the angle) which is winning. They thrunge past you, and for a moment you can see that one of the crews is in front of the other, and then they disappear into the distance. Later you hear (mostly) that the one that was leading won; occasionally you hear that the trailing crew made a sudden charge and won narrowly; you wish you'd seen it.

Standing at the start is better. You watch the spray and the effort and hear the noise as two crews disappear into the distance. Otherwise, as above.

At the finish, generally, you see one crew leading the other, and they win. Occasionally there's a late charge, which is fun. Then it's all quiet until the next procession, where the leading crew again wins.

Now take six-lane racing. All the above applies, except that the crews are so far away that you can't even see which one is which, and in addition, you get no feeling of the power and effort that's going in.

I'm being provocative here, as a rower I like to watch racing, though I wouldn't put fuel in the car for the six-lane format.

But if my non-rowing friends want my opinion then here it is; watch it on TV and fast-forward liberally.

Alan Clarence

Alan Clarence is a physical therapist in Adelaide, Australia. A thread on the Masters Rowing International Facebook group was started by him with this short story.

Who Needs Oars Anyway?

I've caught crabs, I've tipped out. I've somersaulted a boat. Crashed into another boat. Put my gates back to front and put a bow and stroke oars on the wrong side. I've seen a guy snap a $1,000 oar and raced a guy who had his dog in the boat with him. I've come last by so far that everyone else was gone by the time I crossed the finish, then took a State Title a month later. But until I started coaching juniors, I had never, I mean NEVER seen rowers go out and forget to take their oars with them!

Which netted these replies:

Joseph N Grima
Must be a juniors thing. I was 40 the other guy 18!

Lynore Abbott
We did take the oars to the dock... but we left them there and pushed out. At least no one immortalised our stupidity on video,

Ian Carmody

I saw two first graders put their sculls in the swivels but they were facing the bow. Can't remember if they rowed off. Heaps of red faces. At least the kids were laughing.

Philip Petch

I have seen a novice crew pile into their racing eight at their first regatta without any oars. There was a loud shriek and nine pairs of heels in the air. It took a long time to get that 8 out again: there was a strong breeze and chop against the pontoon which made it difficult to empty the boat. I suspect they never made that mistake again!

Ian Hodge

Got to the regatta with my doubles partner and realized that in our haste to ensure that all the boats were packed correctly onto the trailers, (the only time we had volunteered for this duty) we had forgotten to take our own boat!

Craig Ryan

I remember the bowman of a school's first eight getting in backwards and trying to figure out why there was no one in front of him!

Elliza McGrand

Elliza McGrand is a keen appreciator of the history of rowing. She rows in Portland, Oregon, USA.

In agreeing to send me this Rowing Tale, she described it as "OK, let's have our great rowing knucklehead moments put down on paper." And so I have obliged.

Secret Vermont Boatmakers

A few years ago I was looking at rowing shells and I was also going to Vermont for rowing-related reasons. I was new to Facebook and saw what I thought was an interesting FB mention about a boat maker – "Remador VT."

Remador VT? I thought.

I was going to a place in Vermont that did rowing-related day trips, maybe we could go there? (Please Goddess-of-Rowing, let me not have suggested it).

Then I got a little indignant - there was a Vermont-based boat maker and we weren't visiting?? Maybe they made beautiful wooden boats! Why isn't Vermont supporting their local boat makers?!

I am sorry to report that I asked a number of people about this boat maker; if they'd ever rowed one of those Remador VT boats and what they thought of them.

No takers.

I believe I even FB friended Remador VT to get more info. I couldn't understand why they never posted anything about the boats they made, what was up with that!? I researched on the net to find out more about their boats and couldn't figure out why the results I got were so odd.

For those now dear to my heart who are equally confused, it turns out "Remador" means rower in Spanish.

It isn't a boat company, it's a group for Spanish rowers. I don't know why they added "VT" after the word :Remador."

It took me weeks to figure this out.

Have you ever thought you'd like to row in a traditional wooden single scull? This is how one athlete took the plunge and made their own racing single - probably the only wooden boat to have been made in Australia this century.

Building A Wooden Rowing Shell

Building a wooden rowing shell

I learnt to row at Oxford in the early 1980s at a time when wooden racing shells were the state of the art. I was totally impressed by the boatmen that the colleges employed to maintain their various fleets. They were remarkable craftsmen and I used to love visiting their workshop to watch them make repairs and learn about setting up the rigging for optimal performance of the racing shell.

During the 1980s there were remarkable and substantial changes in the racing boat industry. The shells were replaced with carbon fibre technology and the wooden oars were also replaced with carbon fibre shafts. Technology and computer-aided design have led to boats produced today which are relatively cheap and almost perfect in design and construction.

There is, however, something about a wooden rowing shell. Nobody makes them commercially anymore and the craftsmanship and body of knowledge associated with their construction is rapidly disappearing. It is very hard to find a skill base by searching on the internet or in libraries.

I thus set about to build a wooden racing shell. This in retrospect was ambitious, since I had never built a boat before and had very minimal woodworking skills and knowledge. The first task was to build a shed that was sufficiently long to cater for the project. This happened to coincide with our plans for the house, so that worked out well, although the extra few metre's length took some convincing! I then happened to find an old shell in gross disrepair that was gathering dust at the top of a neighbouring rowing club's boatshed. After a little negotiation, I was able to take it away with blessings and lots of wishes of "good luck"!

I then spent the next year or so taking thousands of measurements and making drawings for the construction of a new boat. As if this wasn't challenging enough, the old shell was built for a small lightweight person and I needed to make some modifications in length and width to accommodate my heavier stature. I did this by making similar measurements of the boats that I currently row and was able to make appropriate adaptations (at least, I hoped they would work!).

The drawing stage was very interesting as I began to understand the basis for the design. I found it intriguing how all the measures came together to make comprehensible patterns. Often, it would be very challenging to make appropriate measurements and some innovative solutions had to be sought. By the end of the drawing phase, I was well and truly over-measuring and eager to start building. I had to source some good wood and found a brilliant local supplier whose stock was of superb quality.

It was actually quite hard to start, as I did not know where to begin and I had no instructions or advice to follow. So I just started by laying out the deck superstructure on a flat wooden base built on the concrete floor. I soon learnt the necessity for accurate measuring and how to work with curves. I found it hard to get the lines just right but had fun eventually achieving a reasonable level of symmetry.

One of the best gadgets I bought during this project was a laser line which gave me straight lines for setting up the centre line without having to use string. It was invaluable throughout the whole project. I used the TechniglueCA two-part structural epoxy adhesive for all the joins as it had a perfect consistency and was really easy to use. No screws or tacks were used. Once the deck frame was completed, I moved the structure on to a series of three work-benches that I built to the same height and level and began the next stage to mount the keel.

I knew at some stage I would need to insert the moulds to shape the shell, but I didn't know at what stage these should be inserted. So I concentrated on building the framework for the seat, the cockpit and the supporting struts for the keel. The molds for shaping the shell were then inserted after the keel was installed on the deck upside down.

This approach worked well and the framework was finally completed. The mould shapes had to be constructed in such a way that they could be removed from the framework once the ply shell had been added. This took a lot of trial and error and I was glad that I had waited until this stage to fine tune their shape and attachment for easy removal. They were fixed firmly in place by small G-clamps so that there would be no structural damage when taking them out. I rehearsed placement of the G-clamps to ensure they could be removed.

The shell section was very challenging. My first attempt was a complete failure! I used a 3mm hoop pine marine ply and started experimenting with how to shape the ply and bend it appropriately to fit the molds. I quickly learnt that this three-ply was too thick and the section I completed ended up twisting and contorting the

58

superstructure! It was very disheartening pulling it apart and starting again. At this stage I decided I really needed expert advice. So I rang Alan Phillips who owns Race1 boats, a successful building firm making carbon fibre racing shells for high-performance rowing competition. He has supplied our rowing club with these boats for the last two decades.

I asked him if he knew anyone who knew about building wooden shells. As it turned out, he did his apprenticeship building wooden shells for Sergeant and Burton, an old firm who was a major producer in Australia in years gone by. It turned out that Alan was probably one of only a handful of people left in Australia who had experience in this trade. So I invited him for a Sunday lunch and we spent hours in the shed with him showing me how to do the shell and he also gave me some tips on working with some of the tools. It was a great day and I really appreciated his help.

These boats were traditionally made from red cedar ply due its strength and light weight, and they looked very nice. However, this could only be obtained at an enormous cost by importing from the USA. I managed to find 1.2mm three-ply from my local supplier which was made of birch. This would mean that my boat would be an unusual golden light brown colour, which I thought would be great. The first stage was to cut the three-ply into narrow widths that would be sufficient to cover the curvature of the mould shapes with sufficient left-over to allow for the distorted shape from twisting the wood around the curvature. These were then joined as scarf joints (another challenge in its own right with 1.2mm ply) before attaching to the boat. The lengths were then fitted and glued to the side rails. Then they could be bent over the keel. The shell lengths of ply were first glued to gunwales under stress of shape before cutting the centre line for the join and held in place with multiple straps and small lengths of timber.

The centre of the keel line is where a neat join is required from each piece of three-ply. The centre line cut was made in small sections 15cm at a time by marking and cutting grooves into the line prior cutting the joint line with a sharp blade.

This is achieved by cutting a small section with a sharp blade until the centre line is observed. Then move down a further 10-15cm to the next point where another incision is made. You can then join the two marks by a straight edge ruler to achieve the line for cutting using a sharp Stanley knife. It is thus possible to achieve the shaping of the three-ply and accurate determination of the centre keel line for joining. This was difficult and challenging but extremely rewarding when you step back and actually see the hull shaped after gluing.

Whilst the boat was upside down, I completed the hull preparation and glassing. Having suffered a little despair earlier with the three-ply, I was now in full gear to complete the boat and row it. This had taken about three and a half years as I didn't get that much time to work on it during the week.

As I was doing the final sanding prior to laying the glass, a bird flew into the shed, became very excited and deposited a drop on the middle of my newly completed shell! I couldn't believe my luck – birds have never done this before and to add insult to injury, it had been eating red mulberries! I now have a little stain on my shell which was impossible to remove because I could not sand it off due to the very thin layers in the ply. Fortunately it now looks like a reasonable natural wood blemish in colour. I made extensive efforts to clean the shed and remove dust and particles which could affect the glassing process. I was pretty happy with the outcome until I finished the whole boat and took it outside on a bright sunny day and found a black dog hair embedded in the resin layer from my constant companion in the shed!

The rest of the boat was a pleasure to complete. The internal boat structure was treated with multiple layers of International Everdure two-part epoxy primer and wood sealer, which was easy to use and extremely effective. The remaining exposed woodwork in the cockpit area and gunwales were also primed with the Everdure and finally coated with International Perfection Plus two-part polyurethane varnish. The fore and aft decks were covered in a stretchy plastic material that was the closest I could find to the original 'canvas' material used. This was recommended by Alan Phillips – thanks again to his advice for applying this evenly and smoothly. It is held on by a very strong double sided tape and then the edges were covered in a strong black tape to completely seal the covering. The seat and rails were supplied from Ausrowtec (Australia) and the foot stretchers and riggers were custom built and supplied by Rowfit International (Australia).

After completion, I had to wait many weeks for an opportunity to launch the boat and test it. This was mainly associated with a bout of windy weather. Finally I had an opportunity to take it out in very flat and perfect conditions. To my surprise, it was comfortable and it rowed straight – this was my biggest fear as I have been in boats that flex too much, or the rigging is not set up properly or the boat is misshapen. It also took my weight and it was a delight to row – probably because I had made it, but also there is a feeling that it works in a different way because of the way it is designed to cater for the strengths of wood relative to carbon fibre.

I now have a bigger appreciation of these racing shells and the skills of the boat builders who built the wooden ones in the past, and also those who construct the amazingly precise boats of today.

It also makes me realise how much I don't know about boat design, construction and performance.

My next boat will not be another racing shell! In fact I have already started working on the Ocean Pointer from Stimson Marine and it is so nice having step by step instructions, drawings and a plan!

Istvan Nemeth

Istvan Nemeth is the founder of Bont Rowing Shoes and has been a keen rower in Sydney since childhood. In this tale he recalls the moment when he first fell in love with the sport.

Rowing, We Know!

Rowing is one of the most amazing sports on the planet.

You know we get to go out there and watch the day being born. Every morning we're out there.

And you know, when people say to me, what is the absolute most relaxing thing, most beautiful thing I've done, I'll always go back to this one particular row.

When I was a kid, I would have been 16 or 17. I was out there by myself in a boat and it was like glass.

All I could hear was that hollow sound of when your oars are just entering the water and the slide.

That was a few years ago and the memory will always be with me. I'm 52 now. It's stayed with me all that time.

So yeah, that's it, it's an amazing sport.

I would just love to see that being shared more and just people in the sport at all levels just joining in and enjoying.

James Rowe

James Rowe hails from Greenthorpe, New South Wales in Australia. With his wife, June, he founded not for profit Lachlan Aquatic Recreation Collective Inc. He's been in the sport a long time.

Rowing Toys

Back in the day, Haberfield Rowing Club (now UTS Haberfield) in Sydney, Australia used to have coat hooks in the changing rooms.

They were set either high or low (for young coxswains).

At the time, the lightweight rowers were known as 'toys' in the colloquial slang.

As a young coxswain I enjoyed having my coat on the hooks marked toys.

Scott Roswell

Scott is a South African Rower and coach. He shared this frustrating post about a crew with potential who couldn't overcome their egos and so failed to achieve.

Flipping The Eight

I once had a high school crew flip an eight. Good athletes, but all eight thought they could walk on water and were almost uncoachable.

It was their high point in rowing and happened a couple of weeks after the high school season started.

Basically, they managed an eight-man crab when they went rogue in a practice and then decided they could do full power pieces and didn't need a coach.

All were known athletes from other sports and on paper, they should have been fast.

They got a few days of shore leave after that event and once it ended, were only humbled for a short period, but not enough that they ever became as decent a crew as they could have been.

Not my favourite group. None repeated in the club or the following season...

Life... rowing... lessons.

Martin Sharrock

Martin Sharrock took up rowing later in life, fascinated more by his 13 year old daughter's determination than performances in the sport. Addiction soon followed to the technical and physical challenges of rowing, especially in the single scull.

Almost Garmin Gone

I don't have a stroke coach computer, but I do have a Garmin watch.

Quick glances down to my right wrist at the tap down tell me the essentials of stroke rate and time per 500. I always wear it in training and sometimes during races.

On regatta day recently on Lake Karapiro, New Zealand, I backed down my single scull into the start, got attached and pressed the button on the watch.

Ready to go.

A mediocre start was somewhat recovered by the first 250 meter mark.

Then time froze; in my brain rather than on my watch.

The Garmin was sitting there on top of my wrist, at the finish of the stroke, but something did not feel right. A downward glance at my frozen arms revealed an open strap with the watch balanced precariously and loosely on my wrist.

So what to do when time starts again?

Fast arms away and even faster "watch away" into the depths of the lake?

Continue to sit frozen whilst my competition push away?

On reflection, I think I quickly grasped both handles in my right hand and carefully grabbed the Garmin with my now free left hand.

Now what? Frozen once again in my own private universe. I remember the stroke rate now said zero which was not useful in the middle of a race. I tossed the watch down into the footwell and returned to what I was supposed to be doing. It did cross my mind that now would not be a good time to capsize.

I didn't do well in the race. I did however have a perfect excuse. I even had proof after the race! My obedient Garmin watch that I was destined to own for a while longer recorded everything. Stroke rate from start to 250m: 32. Stroke rate from 250m to 1000m: zero.

Rebecca Caroe

Rebecca Caroe leaned the craft of single sculling on the Tideway in London, UK. The river flows fast and to race it well takes a lot of "lore" and practice navigating the eddies around the bridges as well as knowing where not to cut corners.

A Racing Dilemma

I was getting quite good at single sculling and beginning to enjoy racing.

The Scullers Head was the big test - a full Boat Race course going with the outgoing tide. I was keen, fit and practiced. Definitely gunning for a personal best - not really likely to win but I had goals.

Coming around the last big bend at Hammersmith Bridge, the river suddenly changed. It was a direct head wind and the wind was fighting the outgoing tide. A hideous surface chop of wavelets was building.

I was not too discomforted at first because the waves were small, but I realised after I'd passed the Harrods Depository and was into the final 2,000 meters that those waves were just going to build and build right through to the finish line.

Time to reassess my racing line.

I stole a look over one shoulder - whitecaps. Over the other shoulder - possibly some shelter near the bank. Decision time - stay out in the stream or head for slack water with slightly less wave action?

I made up my mind and did one last look over my left shoulder. And as I turned my head back, I'd moved too fast. My contact lens had popped out of my eye and was sitting on my cheek just below my eyelashes.

I have small eyes and in those days wore hard contact lenses. The action of squinting into the distance as I looked around and probably blinking, while turning my head had caused my eyelid to close on the edge of the lens.

What to do?

My brain was running a complex, multivariate calculation. The replacement lens was £80, the race entry was £25, I had just overtaken Vicky (who'd been to the Commonwealth Regatta and was a much classier athlete than me). Should I stop racing and put the lens into the bottom of the boat - or into my sock? Or should I throw caution (and my contact lens) to the wind and keep going?

I really did not want Vicky to overtake me again. I'd expended a lot of effort to get past her. She wouldn't know that I had stopped... But...

Reader, I rowed on.

What would you have done?

Niall Bates

Endurance rowers are a class apart. Niall Bates is not only an erg marathoner, he's a multiple time marathoner. Respect doesn't even cover my admiration.

Once More Unto The Breach

Rowing a marathon distance on an erg is hard, but what's really hard is training for a 42.2km row. Rowing a marathon "only" lasts around 3 hours. It's tough on the body but is relatively short, very goal specific and most importantly marks the end of the brutal training program you've just undertaken. Training for a marathon row - now that's a whole other world of pain. 2-3 months of 60-90 minute, soul-sapping erg sessions. The program is relentless - a long row every 2 days. The day you're rowing, the session is like a black cloud hanging over you all day. It is incredible the things you can find to do instead of doing your training row. But eventually you do it. The day after your session your legs are dead and there's that unmistakable feeling of dread that you have to do it all again tomorrow.

I did my first marathon distance back in 2012 as a simple "I wonder if I can do this?" challenge.

After a bit of research online on the topic, the name Eddie Fletcher kept appearing. I found his program which on paper seemed easy enough - 12 weeks of 3 sessions per week, none longer than 90 minutes - that was just 36 rowing sessions and then I'd be marathon fit. "How hard can that be?" I thought to myself. About 45 minutes into the first session I realised exactly how hard it was going to be. We all know the erg is as much a test of mental strength as physical fitness, but the longer distances really tested the body as much as the mind. The program quickly ramps up to 90 minute sessions which really hurt. It's hard to describe the feeling of having just rowed a 45 minute piece close to flat out and then setting off on another one after just a 4 minute break.

Eddie has a real talent for turning an already aggressively mind-numbing, heart-breaking machine into a whole new world of pain. It's like Chinese water torture whilst listening to Jedward's greatest hits on repeat.

I've done the program a total of 4 times. The first marathon I completed in 3 hrs 08 mins and I was happy enough just to successfully complete the distance. It's a strange feeling of rowing into the unknown when you key in the distance of 42,197m into the machine, never having rowed more than a half marathon distance before.

Your mind is full of doubts - "Am I ready for this?", "How am I going to now double the longest distance I've ever rowed before?" and of course "Why am I doing this?".

But you realise that the goal marathon pace is sufficiently slower than the pace you've been training at so when you reach 20k feeling pretty fresh you start to believe the program actually works. By the time I completed the distance, I was certainly tired but felt I could do quite significantly better if I had just pushed myself a little harder both in training and in the row itself.

Despite the usual promise of "never again", just 12 months later a friend asked if I fancied having another go at it as he was thinking of doing it and we could have a go together. And so I spent another 3 months with my 'new best friend, Eddie'.

True to my word, I pushed harder this time with more aggressive rates in the training sessions. It was brutally hard on my body and completely exhausting. After one of the 90 minute rows we had friends over for dinner and I literally fell asleep at the table! Thankfully we knew them well and we explained after what was going on so it wasn't a diplomatic incident!

My target this time was sub 3 hours which was quite significantly faster than my last row but the training had gone well so I knew I was capable of doing it. When marathon day came along I was absolutely dreading the row. In fact I very nearly stopped after 10k, reasoning with myself that no one on the planet cared whether I completed the row or not so why was I bothering? It was a pretty good argument to stop, but I carried on regardless. As someone once put it - "You can quit as many times as you like as long you keep on rowing". This time I did it in 2 hrs 57 mins and was completely drained by the end. Job done, never again.

The third time I followed the program was for a very different reason. Ever since I had taken up rowing at University aged 19 I had been absolutely fascinated by ocean rowing. Rowing 2k was so incredibly difficult, how was it even possible for humans to row 6,000 km? It took many years to get the time, funds and motivation in place and in 2016 I finally signed up with a boat to do the crossing in 2017.

When it came to training it was a long and tough process. Weights, on the water rowing, erg training, flexibility, core strengthening were all on the agenda. When it came to the erg training I returned to an old but familiar marathon training program - "Hello old friend, it's been a long time."

This time though I did the program, but not the marathon itself. Rowing a marathon is a dramatic strain on the body which really empties you to the core. I described the last 10k to someone as like rowing a 10k when you've got the flu. Every stroke is an effort. You dare not think about more than the next stroke as if you contemplated the 1000 or so strokes still remaining it would be enough to stop you dead in your tracks. Just get the next stroke right and then worry about the rest later. To undergo such a physically traumatic experience before setting off to row an ocean seemed a bad idea, so this time I completed the training program but didn't row the marathon itself - just 6,000km across the Atlantic instead! I'm happy to say, we rowed our successful crossing in 48 days.

The fourth (and current) time I'm doing the program is to take part in this year's Tour de Lac Léman race in September. It's an annual rowing race on Lake Geneva - one lap of the lake which equates to around 160km (100 miles in old money). It's apparently the longest fresh-water rowing race in the world.

So, to get myself into the required physical shape I fall back on a program that by now I know oh so well. "Oh it's you again". Midway through the plan, there was one particular incident that sums it all up for me.

One day, I had a 90 minute row looming on the horizon which I really, really didn't want to do. "Put it off till tomorrow - no one cares" said the voice in my head. I was tempted, very tempted, but I knew I should really do the session. I found so many things to do that day other than do the training session, it was quite remarkable - tidied the basement, did the accounts, fixed the dicky door handle that had been broken for months. But then, despite my best efforts, I knew I had to face the music.

Not for the first time, I trudged slowly upstairs, like a condemned man on death row walking his final walk. I readied myself as best I could, sat down on the erg and looked at the session ahead of me. 60 minutes? What the hell? I was sure the session was 90 minutes

73

but no, in week 4 it drops back from 90 minute sessions to 60 minute ones - I couldn't believe my eyes. The condemned man just got a last minute reprieve! I could have cried with relief. And what ensued was the happiest, most enjoyable - sorry, least miserable - 60 minute session I have ever rowed on an erg. I smiled throughout, laughing that it could have been much, much worse.

If a rational, non-rowing person were to read such behaviour they would no doubt, and probably with good reason, suggest rowers are insane. I'm still not entirely sure why we do this to ourselves but at this stage I simply don't know any better.

In terms of the program, the Eddie Fletcher program is brutally harsh but remarkably effective at preparing the rower for a marathon distance. It should come with a health-warning, but we all know rowers wouldn't take any notice anyway.

Despite never having met the man, I feel I have a love/hate relationship with Eddie at this stage. And if ever I do meet him I'll probably feel the desire to kick him in the shins for all the pain he's put me through, but instead will buy him a pint and congratulate him on bringing a whole new level of pain to the sport we love so much.

Lauren Colman

Lauren Colman sculls in the beautiful American Northwest. He describes himself as being 'old enough to have known George Pocock and visited his workshop'. I rowed in high school and college, Princeton University '66-'70, and then was limited to just the Concept2 Model A ergometer until he started sculling a little more than 10 years ago aged 62.

Tale of the Tail of the Lake

The Tail of the Lake is a delightful head race starting in the ship canal and rowing counterclockwise around mile-long Lake Union in Seattle.

In my experience it has always been an adventure.

One year a tug, a large barge with a pile driver, entered the ship canal as the racing started leaving the smallest room for the boats to pass. Another year the wake of a seaplane taking off swamped a women's masters 1x and flipped her into the water. She managed to get back into her boat and finish the race.

Another year a 10 knot southerly wind generated significant waves which bounced off the concrete bulkhead at Gas Works Park at the north end hitting the boats in the last 500 meters with broadside waves making the last 500 meters a real struggle for many boats.

One year a local tribe of Native Americans who have the right to net salmon in Lake Union laid a gill net across the course in the middle of the racing.

A race official hurried to the location and called out to the boats "Go around the buoy! Go around the buoy!" at the end of the net but didn't specify which side of the buoy to go around so some of the boats, me included, chose unwisely and briefly were entangled in the netting.

It has always been an adventure to row the Tail of the Lake, but it's always been a fun race.

Linda Desrosiers & Anne Seeley

Linda Desrosiers and Anne Seeley are long time Bainbridge Island rowers. This is the history of their new club and how a group of masters set themselves the goal of competing in the 2011 San Diego Crew Classic eights regatta. Each athlete tells their story of their rowing journey, accompanied by an inspirational quote.

Note: All sections except as noted were originally self-published in 2011.

Yes, We Have Legs

Prologue (2022)
Linda Desrosiers and Anne Seeley

Bainbridge Island, Washington, lies just over half an hour due west of Seattle, by ferry. It has numerous harbors and inlets and a climate that allows for rowing almost year-round, so you'd think there would be somewhere that a group of would-be rowers could establish a base. Many tried but none prevailed - until the year 2000 when a group of passionate and determined high schoolers undertook a detailed survey of the island's shoreline and located a couple of possible sites.

Meetings were held, potential coaches were contacted, and, with the support of parents and a few experienced Masters rowers, a beach on the south end of the island was identified as possibly workable. Permission to use it, for the time being, was given by the homeowners – and thus was born Bainbridge Island Rowing.

A Juniors program started that spring, taking to the water in two very old eights donated by the University of Washington. A group of potential Masters, most of whom had never rowed before, looked on and decided to start their own first Learn-to-Row session that summer.

A year later, in June 2001, 20 women showed up for Learn-to-Row-and-Race, a program that would, over the course of eight weeks (rowing three days a week starting at 5:30 a.m.) teach the rudiments and fundamentals of rowing and culminate with a novice race at the annual summer regatta on Green Lake, in Seattle, in early August.

Some called it quits after that, while many others were fired up to continue.

Over the next few years, the fledgling club had its ups and downs. Interest in rowing grew among both Juniors and Masters. A variety of coaches came and went. The equipment situation went from bad to worse. At one memorable practice, the safety boat had to be towed in by an eight.

In 2002, permission was granted by the City of Bainbridge Island to move the growing fleet to the city-owned Waterfront Park, on Eagle Harbor, roughly midway down the east side of the island. The harbor was sheltered but crowded, and boat traffic included the frequent ferries from Seattle that came and went from early morning until late at night.

The initial 'boathouse' was a covered rack, on a slope, below a pair of public tennis courts, and we never knew quite what would be going on when we showed up in the morning. Vandals once damaged several pieces of equipment. Electric wiring in the boats was unreliable—the salt water didn't help. The Boston Whaler used as a safety launch often failed to start. Wet launching in February chilled our toes.

Eagle Harbor is ringed on three sides with many fine waterfront homes whose occupants did not always appreciate the amount of shouting involved at 5 a.m. On at least one occasion, the said shouting brought the local police down to greet a boat returning to shore after practice. And for a time, the fisherman neighbor of one of the Masters drove the safety boat just so rowers could be on the water.

And yet, the rowing programs continued to multiply: Junior Boys, Junior Girls, Masters Men, Masters Women, Learn-to-Row. Early morning, mid-morning, and evening. The Juniors started racing – regionally and then nationally. The Masters wanted in.

A group of early morning women wanted to get serious, but it was hard to find an experienced rowing coach who would hang around a small island for little or no pay. Summers were most successful with some great college rowers coming in to coach. The women entered regattas on and off, and a few who made sculling a priority in fact did quite well at many regattas, but even with a lot of spirit, the eights often just ended up DFL [dead fricking last]..

All that ended in the fall of 2010, we got organized, set a goal to row in the famous San Diego Crew Classic, found an experienced and energizing coach, and set out on the path. We trained, we raced, and we had a great time. We even made it into the finals after a challengingly windy heat. These are our stories.

In the Beginning... Linda Desrosiers

In November of 2010, 33 Masters Women sweep rowers from Bainbridge Island were surveyed for interest in rowing the San Diego Crew Classic in April 2011. Many jumped right on the Yes button. Some had to send regrets but vowed to do it another year. Others were so new that they just couldn't see it in their foreseeable future (little did they know!).

By December 11th, 11 women started training to find the power necessary to be in a race of this category. And we were lucky to find Grant Dull available and willing to take on the task of coaching us through to achieving this goal. He provided us with workouts that started immediately. He didn't just send them though — he was there to do them with us! He asked for a 2K test time from everyone within the first week. We did it.

We were told we had to go to Ergomania on February 5th. We did it. And everyone who went to Ergomania improved their test score, some quite dramatically. We were already getting stronger.

Our on-water time began in the dark freezing morning hours in February. By March 1st, Grant had identified the race line-up and alternates, and we were on our way. The 11 women were asked to write something about rowing, what it meant to them, how they got started, or about this recent training. This was an easy task. Somehow rowing is very connected to the heart and very easy to write about.

This book is our thank you to Grant.

Barb Emel – Two Seat

"Oh... the Places you will go
You'll get mixed up, of course, as you already know. You'll get mixed up with many strange birds as you go. So be sure when you step. Step with care and great tact and remember that... Life's A Great Balancing Act. And will you succeed?
Yes! You will, indeed! (98 and 3/4 percent guaranteed.)"
Dr. Seuss

To be mentally and physically challenged to the point of maniacal amusement in any sport at my age has been the highlight of passage into my 50s and 60s. It has been a fiercely personal challenge to experience the rhythm within and to be able to blend it with others. The beauty of that rhythm often overwhelms me, driving the passion. The stillness of the surroundings, the rush of the water, and the click of the oars are mesmerizing.

Thank you to all my rowing mates for the camaraderie, and thank you to our coach with the keen eye and the obvious passion for this most wondrous sport.

Callie Sheehan – Four Seat

'The sea does not reward those who are too anxious, too greedy or too impatient. To dig for treasures shows not only impatience and greed, but lack of faith. Patience, patience, patience is what the sea teaches. Patience and faith.

One should lie empty, open, choiceless as a beach—waiting for a gift from the sea.'

Anne Morrow Lindbergh

Rowing always surprises me.

I joined Learn-to-Row on Bainbridge to spend time with my daughter the summer before she left for college. We enjoyed our time, and when she moved on, I was surprised to find I was anxious to learn more about rowing. As I focused on learning the physical and mental aspects of the sport, I was also trying to take in all the new terminology and seasonal differences.

I loved starting the day being silent in the dark, working on improvement and taking time to focus only on rowing, saving work, family, and other commitments for other times of the day. And then when I found myself at my first regatta, I looked around and was surprised to find all these dear friendships that had developed.

A year or two after I started rowing, my teenage son joined the junior team. I was surprised again by the depth of his personal

81

development that comes from being part of a team while he also worked on his individual goals. The bond with the other parents of Junior rowers surprised me too, I remember the day I realized we were a community. Joining the Board has surprised me in ways I hadn't expected. We are clearly building something and we are surrounded daily by caring, hard-working and talented people.

And once again I am surprised that this fabulous group of ladies decided to enter the San Diego Crew Classic. We have all made it a priority in our busy lives, our coach has pushed and inspired us and we are consistently working hard, and our plans are taking shape. While I knew we'd enjoy the team camaraderie, I am surprised by the moving forward of the team as a whole, enjoying the moment but recognizing the longer-term rewards. While I don't yet know what San Diego holds for us, I do know I love surprises!

Grant - thank you for sharing your knowledge and experience with all of us. While it is exciting to see our near-term goal quickly approaching, the real gift is what you've done for us in the long run. There will undoubtedly be lasting impacts for years to come. The way you share so selflessly is truly inspiring.

Carrie Holloway – Seven Seat

I got into rowing when I transferred to SPU to get my teaching certification. A friend talked me into going to a crew meeting with her. She ended up quitting early on, but for me, from the minute I got into that seat I was hooked! I rowed with SPU for two years.

Then 20 years later at a BHS staff party, I heard Ann Munro talking about rowing on BI. I started back that summer and then joined the Masters in the fall of 2006. I felt nervous walking in that first early, dark morning, but everyone was so friendly and welcoming, I was at ease right away. I had found my path to bliss. I love the physical aspect of rowing, the whole- body workout. I continue to love and respect the people I row with and enjoy the type of people who are attracted to rowing. I love the mystery of rowing; what factors combine to make a superb row versus an okay row? I love that it's a thinking person's sport.

This winter I have enjoyed working harder than ever with a goal of racing at the end. It's my fellow rowers who keep me showing up at the gym and on the water at o'dark thirty. I appreciate Grant's insights and his ability to be challenging, but not judgmental and not biased. Thank you, Grant, for sharing your time and talents with us!

Cathy Fawley – Three Seat
"Mental will is a muscle that needs exercise, just like muscles of the body."
Lynn Jennings, World champion runner

In 2009, a group of girlfriends got together and wrote a bucket list of the things that each of us wanted to try or learn before we got too old. I had rowing on my bucket list. In summer 2009, I signed up for a learn-to-row class with a couple of friends, Merry and Susan. Linda was our fearless leader, but she made it oh so fun, and we got hooked. I have always enjoyed exercising outdoors, and being on the water in the early mornings, and sometimes evenings at sunset, have been some of my best outdoor memories of all. I love the views from Eagle Harbor in all directions, the mountains, the Sound, and of course the city lights in Seattle.

And the peacefulness. And the oneness with the other rowers. And now training with Grant and the Masters Women has added a new dimension to my rowing experience, knowing that our hard work, focus and perseverance will make that glide through the water even more satisfying! Thank you, Grant!!

Jackie Syvertsen – Bow Seat

"Natural talent only determines the limits of your athletic potential. It's dedication and a willingness to discipline your life that makes it great."
Billie Jean King

I like the water and love to work out, so I responded to a Learn-to-Row ad in the Bainbridge Review back in 2002. I received a response from Coach Jay. I recall he said something to the effect that, "Yes, we have room for you, be at the launch site at 4:45 am. What -- are you kidding? That's the middle of the night and didn't he know I had requested the later session? But due to lack of interest, he went on to say, the 6:30 am session would not be happening. The coach gave me less than a minute to think about it and here I am.

That first morning was tough. I had no idea what crew was. Okay, sit backwards in a boat with one oar — what? Blade, feather, coxswain — huh? For some reason, I thought it was fun. Terrific ladies who I had never met, willing to be silly and try something challenging together.

Grant, I am thrilled that you have taken the challenge to work with us again. You have been a positive mentor by your inspiration, creating and actually doing 'da' workouts for the week along with us. I feel good and strong and worthy of the races before us. This will be a great season and a good design for all Masters seasons to come. Thank you so much.

Jane Stewart – Stroke Seat

"Rowing a race is an art not a frantic scramble. It must be rowed with head power as well as muscular power. From the first

stroke all thoughts of the other crew must be blocked out. Your thoughts must be directed to you and your own boat, always positively, never negative. Row your optimum power every stroke, try and increase the optimum.

"Men (women) as fit as you, when your everyday strength is gone, can draw on a mysterious reservoir of power far greater. Then it is you can reach for the stars. That is the only way champions are made. That is the legacy rowing can leave you. Don't miss it."

George Pocock

In the fall of 1974, I was a sophomore at the University of Washington. I decided I wanted to be part of a team sport. The only thing I could do outside of running was swimming. I found my way to the pool and met the women's swim coach who politely asked if I had ever swam competitively. My answer was "no, but I wouldn't mind trying"... to which he said, "Why don't you try crew? They take people who have never rowed before."

I had no idea what rowing was about but decided to give it a try! I found my way to Conibear Shellhouse and started on an adventure that has changed my life. In the four years I rowed at the University of Washington I saw the impact of Title 9 and what it did for women's sports. It was a rough road as many traditions were being challenged and we were not always met with open arms. As rings true with so many things, it was the people that made the difference. Many of the women I rowed with during that time I am still close friends with and hold a special bond.

Three years ago, I decided it was time to get back in a boat! I joined Bainbridge Island Rowing and have found while some things changed, such as no more wooden boats or oars, much has remained the same. It is a fantastic sport and as before it continues to attract some of the finest people around! I love being out on the water, it has a calming effect on one's being, while the challenge of rowing and striving for the perfect stroke continues to be a joy!

I am so appreciative of this opportunity to row once again at the San Diego Crew Classic, I rowed 4 seat in 1978. I don't remember how we did, other than it was a lot of fun, and yes it was sunny and warm!

I want to thank the 10 other women for making the commitment to train and inspire each other to work hard! How I wish we could change rowers during a race as I would love to see all of us rowing in San Diego! I feel we all have won in what we have accomplished in the way of strength, endurance, improved technique and sheer will to take on a regatta this early and far away!

Grant, thank you for stepping up to the task of coaching us! You have done a fantastic job of working with us; your patience and expertise is greatly appreciated.

Ready All... Row!

Linda Desrosiers – Five Seat

"You gain strength, courage and confidence by every experience in which you really stop to look fear in the face. You are able to say to yourself, "I lived through this horror. I can take the next thing that comes along." You must do the thing you think you cannot do."

Eleanor Roosevelt

I signed up to learn to row when BIR had a booth at the Farmers' Market in the spring of 2002. This decision turned out to be much more fun than I ever could have imagined. Some of the women training for San Diego I've known that long too. Who knows if our paths would have ever crossed any other way. I am very grateful for the friendships that have developed over the years. This opportunity to train with this group of dedicated women has pushed me to a new level of commitment in exercise. It's so much easier to pop to action in the morning knowing others are doing the same thing!

Thank you Grant for saying yes!

Marilyn Tsolomitis – Six Seat

Oars Balance Life

Balance
Rhythm
Drive
Recovery
Repeat
With effort and with ease
Swinging
Together the things
Worth sacrifice and hard work
Moving swiftly
In a direction
To a place
You do not see
Until it has passed
Life
Gliding on the surface
Of calm waters
And of waters too rough to be safe
Be assured
We are in this together
Oar locked
In the pursuit
Of sweet strokes

Whose mutual efforts dig deep
Crab
To be celebrated with champagne
Not salty water
Splashes
From a teammate, yes
A good catch
This sport will catch you
And break you
Down
While building you
Up
Two in two
A pair
A double
Seat mates
Soul mates
An understanding that bonds
Through the sport
That has bonded me
To the water
To the rhythm
The strength

And meaningful purpose　　　　*The ease*
Of friendships　　　　　　　　*The balance*
　　　　　　　　　　　　　　　　Life

Merry Palmer – Alternate (spare)

"What lies behind us and what lies before us are tiny matters compared to what lies within us."
Ralph Waldo Emerson

It began with several friends, a bottle of wine (maybe two) and each of us sharing our bucket list. I have always loved the water and swam competitively in high school. Rowing was not an option for me then. Fast-forward 30 years and I am taking a learn-to-row class with Cathy Fawley and Susan Kelly. I was hooked on the sport at the end of my first class. When Learn-to-Row was over, we talked to Linda and asked - what do we do now? Linda put us in touch with others who were just completing another learn-to-row class, and we started an "intermediate" rowing group in August 2009. That intermediate group consisted of both men and women.

I joined the Masters Women's morning group in the spring of 2010. I rowed in my first regatta that summer. When we started talking about sending an Eight to San Diego, I was in. Can I do it? I think I can! I will follow Grant's workout regimen religiously. I will lift weights and become stronger. I look to the women who are 60-ish as role models. You know what? I took 29 seconds off my 2K erg score!

I am thankful for the great leadership and for the role models I have during this training process. This is just the beginning. 2011 is the first of many years that BIR will attend the San Diego Classic!

Nancy Rignel – Alternate (spare)

"I learn by going where I have to go..."

T. Roethke

We all have our reasons why, and our stories on how we came to rowing. Most of us in mid-life. Some of you know my story. A boating accident on a dark, cold October night in New Hampshire. The OH SHIT moment. But as for the reason—like most humans, mid-life poses the question — 'Is this the beginning of the end?' or 'Is this the beginning?'

After that baptism in Lake Winnipesaukee, I decided that this was 'the beginning'. Every New Year's bucket list I wrote down for years had the same #1 item...'get in shape.' Looking back maybe that meant mentally AND physically. Hmmmm. It was time to stop talking and move on it. I started working with a personal trainer who had just finished a learn-to-row class on Lake Sammamish and she taught me how to erg. Looking back on that time, I wasn't doing it well, but I was doing it! I signed up for a learn learn-to to-row, and I probably wasn't doing it well, but I was doing it!!! I met amazing, strong, committed women. Nine-and-a-half years later I'm still trying to do it well... I'm still doing it! And the women get more and more amazing every day!

If you haven't heard the lake story, you bring the wine and I promise you a really good story!

Susan Kelly – Alternate (spare)

"The motion of the stroke is grace itself, a fluid gesture that propels the delicate shell inexorably forward. The sun is wedging itself into the pale sky. A mist rises off the still water. The shell barely intrudes.

"Eight rowers slide forward on their moving seats, drop their oars as one into the water, catch the momentum and pass it on, release the water and listen for its rush beneath the boat. They

89

repeat this gesture endlessly, captive to its rhythm. Quickly the water smooths over any trace of their presence. And the rowers themselves forget their separateness."
Linda Lewis, Water's Edge

I grew up watching rowers and tailgating at the Head of the Charles. After college, I would park on the Cambridge side of the river and walk over to my office in Boston. I loved hearing the rhythmic kathunk, kathunk as the boats would glide below the Massachusetts Avenue Bridge.

Fast forward a few years to the summer of 2009, Kaitlyn, my daughter, encouraged me to give rowing a try. I took the challenge, signed up for Learn-to-Row, and thanks to a wonderful, kind, patient group of people, I got hooked!

Now I know what Kaitlyn and my son Sean were talking about; I KNOW what it means to be unset!! I love this sport, and am SO very happy to have this opportunity. I thought I would row for fun and relaxation.

I have come to realize that I want to grow, improve, and be truly competitive. I want to win or at least finish knowing I've done my best, haven't let my boat down, and then it will truly be fun. Getting ready for San Diego has helped me realize how much is possible, how far I've come, and how far I can go, all with an amazing group of women and a fabulous coach.

Thanks to our Coxswain, Louise Matoso
noun \ kak-san, - swan

Definition of COXSWAIN
1: a sailor who has charge of a ship's boat and its crew and who usually steers

2: a steersman of a racing shell who usually directs the rowers
Origin of COXSWAIN
Middle English cokswayne, from cok cockboat (a small boat) + swain servant. First Known Use: 15th century

"Louise, you are such a wonderfully focused, calm presence in the boat. THANK YOU for your patience with my catch! Thanks for all you bring to BIR!" (Susan)

"Thanks for being there for us so often in the dark, wet and cold. I really appreciate your quiet confidence and all your insights that have helped us improve our rowing. You're the best. Thank you and please know how very much I appreciate you!" (Carrie)

"Dearest Louise, you make me smile. I love your bright spirit, your spunk, your determination, your positive outlook, your willingness to work hard, your wisdom beyond your years... and, I love the way you lead this group of old gals through the dark morning with a balance of vigor and calm, confidence and fun. It is a big commitment to rise at o'dark thirty and lead us. You do it with grace. Thank you... and to many years of friendship with butts down, feet up on a picnic table, crew races, and general all-around good fun! Love you bunches." (Marilyn)

"We really appreciate your support in helping us reach our goal." (Merry)

"Ma chère Louise. Je vous remercie pour tout ce que vous avez fait pour nous -- merci, merci, merci... And a quote from a favorite contemporary poet /artist, Brian Andreas makes me think of you!"

"Don't you just love it when you get so excited you forget to breathe? The thought of her smiling eyes still makes me laugh. Bien cordialement." (Nancy)

"Thank you so much for sharing your time and energy with us, it has been fun having you in the boat and guiding us so well! You are fabulous!" (Cathy)

"I am so grateful for you, hanging in there with us through all kinds of weather. You have amazing composure and determination, settling for nothing but the best in us. All your encouraging words and constant reminders throughout the row have definitely improved my focus and strength this season. Thank you for agreeing to be part of our San Diego crew, it is obvious you want to win as much as we do. Cheers!" (Jackie)

"Louise, thank you for hanging in there with all of us, you are our eyes, ears and inspiration." (Jane)

"Louise - Your time, energy, commitment and talent have been an amazing gift to our San Diego crew. Thank you so much for all you do for us!" (Callie)

"Louise, Thank you for the generosity of your time, commitment to the sport of rowing, patience with women older than your Mom, and your brilliant coxing!" (Barb)

"You are definitely one of BIR's finest coxswains. You make us so proud. Thank you for sharing your talents with the SDCC crew!" (Linda)

Support

Many people helped us get ready to go to San Diego. Thank you to all the coxswains, rowers, and coaches who made it possible for us to get on the water in early February!

Coxswains: Sean Kelly, Deni Murray, Isabel Vassiliadis, Kaitlyn Kelly, Dillon Byron

Rowers: Anne Seeley, Beth Rabinowitz, Kathy Scanlon, Kirsten Fitzgerald

Coaches: Morgan Seeley, Tom Condon

Organizing: Tracey Schmidt, former BIR rower now with ZLAC. We were so lucky to have Tracey supporting us through all the logistics of taking about 20 people from BIR to San Diego! Thank you, Tracey!

"'Supposing I built a small boat and sailed around the world and when I was a mile from the shore of my home town, and everybody was waiting for me with medals and cameras, I just turned the boat and sailed round again the other way."
Alastair Reid

And we WOULD do it all again! Thank you, Grant!

Race Day addendum (2022) - Linda Desrosiers

It was wonderful to be in San Diego in April. Bainbridge Island had had its usual dark, cold, rainy winter, and spring was slow to come that year.

We got settled in, put the boat together, and went for a warm-up row on a sunny warm day. By race time, a breeze had started and lining up for our race was difficult. We were in lane three out of five lanes, one of the boats came from the eastern US state of Pennsylvania and the other three boats were from California.

After a 10-minute delay at the starting line due to boats having to realign, we had a quick start on the second attempt. The boats took off pretty evenly for the first 500. By 750, Los Gatos jumped way out into open water leaving Marin and Bainbridge still running tight, as lanes two and five struggled to keep up.

By 1,000 meters there was open water between the three front boats and the other two. Marin and Bainbridge battled it out for 2nd place, but in the end, we settled into 3rd and qualified for the final. We were ecstatic to have gotten this far!

93

In the final though, we fell quickly behind and ended up 38 seconds behind the winning boat. It was a wonderful experience for all and many vowed they'd be back! It wasn't all about the race for many – it was the getting there that made it fun. And somehow coming in DFL didn't seem, at least for me, all that bad.

Pre-Final Announcement for the BIR Eight -Anne Seeley

In lane six in this final, having traveled afar from the damp grey Pacific Northwest, and after a winter of early morning erg workouts and icy rows in frigid dark weather, this women's eight from Bainbridge Island Rowing welcomes the warmth of San Diego and the first ever appearance for Bainbridge at this classic west coast regatta.

For all of these women, who range in age from 46 to 63 years old, anticipating the race has been a great excuse to reach out for sunshine after an astonishingly cold, wet winter. For two of the rowers, it's also a row down memory lane. Jane Stewart, today's stroke, raced in San Diego for the UW women's Varsity eight in 1978; seven seat, Carrie Holloway, raced here eight years later, in 1986, as stroke for SPU.

Today's boat is also here to celebrate the 10th anniversary of Bainbridge Island Rowing, a still smallish club established in January 2001, on Bainbridge Island, due west of and a 35-minute ferry ride from Seattle. BIR began with a handful of Junior rowers, whose numbers couldn't even fill an eight. We begged and borrowed boats, on a private beach on the south end of the island. The first group of Masters, some 20 women in all, started rowing the following spring and raced for the first time in the summer of 2002. Under an ever-changing cast of coaches, they've learned, and often relearned, this wonderfully absorbing sport.

Bainbridge Island Rowing now supports a Juniors program of 80 to 100 rowers each season, while more than 70 Masters men and women, aged 35 to 75, participate in a variety of sweep and sculling programs, from the purely recreational to the fiercely competitive. Today's boat is the Dream Big, purchased in 2010 with the proceeds from BIR's first major auction/dinner fundraiser. Go, Bainbridge!

Seen on a T-Shirt in San Diego
She didn't realize how strong she was
Until the day she began
Rowing
It was an epiphany of sorts... She found herself
breathing deeply & with confidence
Taking the world in differently...
She began giving it back just the same
One stroke at a time
with strength and grace and passion

Postscript (2022) - Linda Desrosiers and Anne Seeley
More than ten 10 years after our first San Diego adventure – yes, there were others – only a handful of the women involved above are still rowing. On some, age has taken its toll. For others, life has simply moved into a different lane. But the friendships remain. We remain friends because of our time together and because of the enduring inspiration of our coach and fellow rowers. And, for the record, Bainbridge Island Rowing, which not long ago celebrated its 20th anniversary, has now built a real boathouse at Waterfront Park, where Juniors and Masters programs are thriving.

When time came to review our San Diego stories for publication in *Rowing Tales 2022*, we asked Grant for any thoughts he might have. He deferred, saying rowing was not about the coach, it was always about the rowers. Nonetheless, Grant, we salute you!

Roger Milne

Roger Milne is a multi-lane umpire (referee) from New Zealand who has had the privilege of umpiring Olympic finals. He has shared two collections of tales in this volume, both could be subtitled "what they don't teach you in umpire school"!

Aligners have the job of lining up the bow balls of all the boats in a race.

The World Rowing rules of racing state "Each crew shall have a lane reserved for its own use and shall remain completely (i.e., including its oars or sculls) within this lane throughout the race. If a crew leaves its lane then it does so at its own risk. If it impedes or interferes with any of its opponents or gains any advantage thereby, it may be penalised without prior warning or other notification from the Umpire."

Crews can 'protest' a result if they believe they were impeded by another crew during the race.

Rio 2016 – The Hard Case Bits!

The first Kiwi women's eight ever to qualify for an Olympics saw Kyla Pratt in the bow seat. Her parents own New Zealand's most remote pub, in the metropolis of Whangamomona (population… less than 50, depending on who you ask).

The on-course commentator was Robert Treharne Jones, whom I had previously met at the 2010 Karapiro World Rowing Championships. I gave Robert a piece of paper with the word Whangamomona on it, and he immediately got the pronunciation correct. Imagine the look on the Pratt family's faces in the grandstand, when he used this wee gem of biographical information amid the "on course" commentary!

I had the good fortune to be the "on water" umpire for the mens coxless four final. It was the last race of the finals morning session, and saw Great Britain win well ahead of Australia in second place. AndI will share a story about umpiring that race in a moment.

After umpiring the final, my next job was boat weighing, and the first crew to arrive in the weighing tent, with boat on shoulders and a shiny Olympic Gold Medal around their necks, was Great Britain ... with faces as long as fiddles.

I realised that boat weighing was the last place they wanted to be, and potentially the only hurdle left between the win and celebration. The boat was dumped onto the scales, and I had to do something to break the ice, so I immediately offered them my hand and congratulated them on winning Gold – that cracked it, and smiles resulted...and the boat weight was fine. Australia arrived next, and exactly the same scenario played out.

Sometimes an ounce of humanity really works!

Peace in Rio was ensured by the presence of 60,000 Brazilian troops. The way to the aligners hut was via a pontoon from the footpath, although the footpath area was not accessible to the public. An armed soldier ensured this to be the case. As Judge at the start, I made my way down vertical steps from the footpath to the pontoon, under the watchful eye of the soldier, who indicated a desire to come to the aligners hut for a look.

He handed down his weapon, and I held it while he too climbed down. I felt quite powerful for a few seconds!! I have the photo of him, but not of me...

The men's coxless four finals experience proved to be unforgettable. From about 1,200 meters into the race it was clear Great Britain were going to win, and Australia 2nd, but bronze and 4th were a different proposition.

Republic of South Africa in lane 5 were challenged by a fast (46+) rating Italian crew in lane 6, who came alongside the South Africans at around 1,400 meters, with their oar tips right on the buoy line.

South Africa were also rowing close to the same buoy line. While neither crew transgressed, the distance between their oars must have been no more than 150mm (the width of a buoy). I also know that adjudication of any blade clash was my responsibility as race umpire.

Italy rowed through South Africa and got the bronze. After the finish line, I needed to give the South African crew time to protest before I cleared the race. I purposely counted 60 seconds, and with no sign from South Africa, I raised my white flag in relief – I'm not sure whose heart was pumping faster, the rowers or mine!

Marc-Oliver Klages

Marc-Oliver Klages started rowing as a 9 year old boy in 1978 in Bremen, Germany. I was a club rower during my junior and U23 years. In 1992 I began to coach as a volunteer. Then from 1997 onwards as a professional rowing coach in several rowing clubs and federations in Germany, China, USA, Canada, New Zealand, Belgium, Finland and Denmark.

He shares a diverse range of experiences from his life of rowing and coaching. His rowing nickname is MOK (his initials).

Buoy Hockey and Other Stories

I started rowing in 1978 in a rowing club in Bremen/North Germany. In the early 1980s we were an U15 junior team and competing at local and regional regattas. One thing I still remember from that time is a remarkable race with my partner in a double scull.

We were quite inexperienced in regards of nutrition, in particular pre-race nutrition. My mum had prepared a big food box for the entire weekend. We had our race on Sunday morning and for breakfast I ate a bowl of German potato salad. The ingredients are, beside the potatoes, onions, pickles, salt, pepper and... fatty mayonnaise.

Between breakfast and the race was around one and a half hours. As you can probably imagine, the taste of potato salad during the race is not what you are looking for..... We lost the race by half a meter. My doubles partner was not very happy after the race.

We are still best friends and avoid talking about this little mishap. That was a hard lesson about pre-race nutrition!

Once I was coaching in Montreal, Canada. I had very motivated athletes and it was a pleasure to work with them. Among them was a women's pair. They competed at a regatta in Montreal on the 1976 Olympic regatta course - it's 2000 metres straight, 6 lanes with buoys. After 100 metres they were in front and I was happy about it.

Unfortunately they did not stay in the middle of their lane and began to touch the buoys with their blades. They moved from the left to the right side of the lane and back again. Then they moved out of their lane into the adjacent lane, hitting a lot of buoys during their race. In the end they were the last crew to cross the finish line. After the race we analysed the race and I mentioned that doing two sports together, "buoy-hockey" and rowing, is probably not a good combination and they should decide which sport they prefer to do in the next race.

They never heard about the sport of "buoy-hockey" before and laughed. For the next day they promised to focus on just one sport (rowing) and to stay in their lane. They did a much better race and won a silver medal.

The same year I also coached a lightweight men's pair. We were preparing for the Canadian Henley Regatta.

One morning the bow man came to me and said:"Hey MOK, last night I had a dream. I was the captain of a big ship and I was very proud about it. Then you came, took my captain's hat away and gave me an order to wipe the deck. I was very embarrassed. I was still embarrassed when I woke up."

I just laughed and told him to keep his things in good order.

At Canadian Henley I went to a shop and bought a captain's hat. During the pre race briefing for the race I took the hat out of the bag and put it on the bow man's head.

I said with a smile:"Here you are, captain. No more wiping the deck!" He was very proud. The pair rowed a good race and crossed the finish line in front. He didn't wear the hat to race!

Some years later I was head coach at a rowing club in Bremen, Germany. I had a large junior crew. In preparation for a local long distance race on our lake a junior pair asked me about race strategy.

I told them:"Guys, the best strategy is to row as if the devil is behind you and chasing you."

They totally agreed with it. Then the stroke man asked:"MOK, what shall we do, when the crew behind us is coming closer and trying to overtake us?"

My answer was:"Then you row as if two devils are behind you and chasing you!"

I could see the question marks in their eyes.

Then the bow man turned his head to the stroke man and whispered:"OK, then we double our speed......" Unfortunately the "One-Devil-Speed" was already their limit, some other crews overtook them during the race.

For several years now I have been coaching athletes in the German rowing clubs in South Denmark. So we have Danish and German athletes training together. The rowers here train quite hard. Some of them are a bit more serious, some of them take it rather easier.

There is one very important word in the Danish language. It is "Hygge", which can be translated as a certain kind of "cosiness". This is the very Danish way of life and very important.

I had an U23 rower. He did not train very hard and during the Christmas and New Year holiday he took 5-6 weeks off training. He was a bit surprised about his decreasing erg scores, but did not really care. The results at the spring and summer regattas were exactly what I expected due to his lack of diligence in winter training, but he was not worried about it.

In the second year of our association I asked him:"Hey Simon, you do not train very hard and your results at regattas are not very promising. Most of the races you are crossing the finish line far behind the field. This must feel like a slap in the face. Do you really like this?"

His answer was quite astonishing to me: "Yeah MOK, you are right. Rowing far behind the field is not very satisfying. But the atmosphere of a regatta is so cosy. I like that. And that's why I like to come to regattas and row there."

After that we agreed that I would not bother him anymore with coaching advice and training plan. I said that he could come to practice whenever he wanted. That was a big lesson for me about cultural differences between Denmark and Germany.

One story comes from our Masters group. We have some beginners and some long term rowers in the group and we train and race together. One of the beginners has a background as a cyclist and triathlete, which is a good base for rowing.

We were preparing for a 1k sprint regatta and when we had to put the entries in, we studied the race schedule. It turned out that there was only an hour between the races for the Masters Womens 2x and Masters Mix 4x.

Our endurance athlete said, "It is just two times 4 minutes. I did that kind of interval training many times in cycling and running as well. So this shouldn't be a problem..."

She had never done a 1k race in her life before.

After the first race she gasped, "Holy s**t, I never thought that 4 minutes could be so hard."

Less than an hour later she had her second race of the day. Her succinct comment was just:"My legs and arms are pudding now."

Now every time we enter a regatta, one of the comments is: "It's only 4 minutes..."

Most recently I was racing in a Masters coxless pair against a crew from a friend's rowing club. We were in front and crossed the finish line first. After the race we all met at the bar and had a drink together and analysed our race. The stroke man from our opponent made the philosophical statement. "After the race I thought my arms would hurt, but it was my legs." So true...

Michael Harrison Hsieh

Michael Harrison Hsieh began rowing in 2017 as a masters sculler. He then went back and forth between sweep rowing and sculling at Capital Rowing Club in Washington, DC.

Michael knows masters rowers very, very well. He started this discussion thread and just sat back to watch the fireworks! The first paragraph is his post - the others are all replies. Names have been removed to protect the (not so) innocent!

Eternal Dilemmas

Why are scullers better people than sweep rowers? Discuss. *(leaves the room)*

"Wait. You are both. So can we just always assume the worst about you?"

"Symmetric rowing decreases instances of chronic lumbar pain. Less pain = happier people."

"Scullers can be one person orientated and sweep are more mixers, just saying."

"We tend to be more self-centred but great in bed! (and also makes a quick exit)."

"Why also is port better than starboard? And better looking? Asking for a friend *<also leaves room>*."

"Well I'd say right the opposite... side!"

"You can't drink starboard..."

"I think first you need to define or qualify exactly what you mean by 'better people.' In precisely what way or ways is it suggested that scullers are 'better?'"

"Scullers are more narcissistic. I think that's what he means."
"Says a sweep rower. Or a narcissistic sculler with good self-insight."
"What happens if you do both?"
"Multiple personality disorder."
"I do both, and cox. I must be a hot mess..."
"Is my multiple personality disorder worse if I also row both sides in a sweep boat? I could cox too but I'm not small enough."
"At that point you just reabsorbed your evil twin in utero."

"Neither is better than coxswain so..."
"Coxswains are like football umpires. If you're not good enough to play..."
"I will admit a good coxswain can affect a race."
"No rower with half a brain ever disrespects a coxswain so Imma' giving this a good leaving alone..."

"All scullers are sweep wannabes."

"Simultaneously in tune with both sides of our brain..."

"If you are going to drink a glass of wine, two hands shows better commitment."
"Or greater inebriation."
"So a sculler who also sweeps is schizophrenic?"
"No. Ambidextrous."

"Scullers are stick pullers. Only sweep oars are for real rowers. The Greeks and the Spartans didn't have scullers!"

"Here. Hold this box. Never mind the ticking sound."

"Sweep rowers are very one-sided."
'There are rumours though about some rogues that have mastered the black art of rowing both sides. (Shhh! Let me tell you their secret: they all used to be scullers before...)."

"I've always loved sculling for the solitude. It's like meditating. If there's one thing I can't handle it's people who insist on talking as they row."
"I always talk to The Voices when I'm sculling."
"And the voices talk back to me..."
"Yes. Yes they do."

"This is like pilots vs helicopter pilots... only difference is the ego."

"Because sweep rowers are always one sided, and scullers are more fair and equitable."
"Those that row on both sides are bi-sweptual."

"Well sculling blisters are more symmetrical than sweep blisters, so there's that."

"Scullers are weekend warriors rangdangs and generally make up the ranks of adult learners, river hogs and splashalots. They don't row sweep oar because they didn't learn as teenagers and just think its 'too hard' (like people that learned to drive in their 40's and have never driven a manual car). They therefore have never really learnt to balance a boat. Single scullers are generally loners, socially inept, psychotic and most often sleep with an axe under their pillow."

"I'm very offended by this post. Everyone knows I prefer to sleep with my chainsaw."

"Yes, but what brand of chainsaw? If it's not the socially acceptable brand... We might have to give you the axe."

"Because sweep rowers drop bombs like this and stick around for the discussion."

"... says the coxswain."

"All sweepers should take a turn through the cox seat. Being the brains for 9 people on the water after you've worked a full day is a superpower."

"Ahhhh, the old sweep vs. scullers fight. Well, my cat is smarter than your dog - how you like dat!"

"Scullers are on their way to becoming better people (than they were, before they were banished to solitude). This is of course if they can learn to be accepted back into a team boat."

"Well, National teams train their rowers in singles. Once they make specific boats, then they row sweep or sculling."

"So all rowers start out as good people, and then..."

"More balanced than one sided? Just sayin..."

"Hee hee. I coach, was a cox, rowed sweep and scull. In a pair you can tell who is dogging it not so much in a double. I love all seats but sweep is best. Mic dropped."

"I love this. If you don't like what you do enough to argue that it's the best then why do it. Scullers are lonely insular people who have no friends."

"I'm a sculler and I have you as a friend."

"You're the exception."

"Bow seat rowers have to make up for everyone else's mistakes. Stroke seat rowers should sit behind themselves one day, just to see how hard it is to follow someone who keeps making the same mistakes 35 times a minute. The guys in the middle...... just keep grunting."

"If you can't scull you can't sweep row that's a fact. Well you can but not as effective as a sculler knows how the boat runs."

"Don't confuse this debate with logic."

"The very Greatest Sir Steven Redgrave won the diamonds at Henley before his 5 gold medals at sweep rowing."

"I rest my case."

"To have one you must learn the dark side of the force."

"Young sculling jedi."

"IT'S MEANT TO BE FUN EVERYONE."

"Would make a distinction between a single sculler rather than a crew sculler as there is no such thing a single sweep rower for obvious reasons."

"You must be a single sweep rower."

"Ah but you can be a singled oar rower. Many examples of them."

"Trying to be objective about your question but give up if you are going to be objectionable v rather than objective :)"

"Oh I'm just poking the bear, thanks for... bearing it."

"I read through this thread in a bit more detail and can see now the bear analogy! It's certainly poked a few people but glad to see this particular bear has been poked several times more than anybody else. Very very funny."

Hamish Boyd & Kevin Condon

Hamish travels for work and sent me this story after a visit to Australia.

He rows at Auckland Rowing Club in the masters group and is also the Club Chairman.

A VC is the Victoria Cross - the highest award for bravery in the British and Commonwealth Military. It is awarded for valour "in the presence of the enemy".

The Closest Steering Line

My Uber driver in Sydney this week picked me up after I'd been out on the water with the Glebe Rowing Club masters group. We got talking about rowing and it turned out he'd been a cox many years ago in the UK rowing on the Thames. He told me this amazing little story. I asked if he'd be OK to write it down so that I could share it with you... this is what he sent me.

The year was around 1956.

I was a tiny cox aged 14 at the Thames Rowing Club, Putney, London UK.

I had a very good eye!

My skill was to steer the eight unbelievably close to the bank when the tide was against us – although once the fin did hit something and we sank!

Our coach was Johnny Johnson, who was a bit of a war hero, (I think a VC).

The start of the rowing season always began with a regatta at the Hurlingham Club (in Putney) and then every week flowing up the river until eventually it got to Henley Town and the Henley Town Regatta.

Anyway, on this particular afternoon we were traveling fast going through a bridge at Hurley.

With the oars fully extended we had just inches on either side to spare.

As we sped through, out of the reeds on the other side of the bridge came a clinker rowing boat with a couple and a young boy in the bow. (I remember it being a blind spot.)

It was in the days before lifejackets!!

We hit the boat square on its side at speed causing a big hole.

And the boy disappeared.

The Thames was thick with green sediment – it was hard to see anything below the water line.

One of us dived looking for him. We searched and searched I think for about 5 -6 minutes but could not see the boy for love or money.

The parents were desperate – there was no one else around to help.

So, we decided to give up thinking he could not have survived.

We turned the eight around to help the parents get to the shore.

And as the bow-blade went down for the first stroke and came up again so did the little boy – alive at the end of the oar!

We were of course all relieved!

All I can remember after that was going to Leander Club - the famous rowing club at Henley – when everyone hit the beer – except for me – I was only allowed Babycham!

And it didn't matter how many!

Afterwards, the crew threw me over Henley Bridge! I hope they checked traffic underneath first!

Your friend is very welcome to publish it.

Kevin Condon

And Hamish, I promise it is true!

Rebecca Caroe

Rebecca Caroe thinks she's probably the world's most unlikely rower. The sport came into her life first during an overseas backpacking holiday, this is the story of her first ever Henley.

The Zaniest Regatta in the World

Famously, Australians can take a joke against themselves. From the country that brought you bananas in pyjamas and men in cork hats, I submit a regatta without water as a fine addition to their list of cultural icons.

Roll back a few decades and I was a back packer on my first solo trip. I visited Australia because my grandmother was born there and while in Adelaide I had tea with a doughty elderly lady who had known my great grandmother. She was delighted to give me a small sepia photo of Gwendoline. She also suggested I visit Alice Springs - the desert oasis in the Australian outback. I took her advice and suffered the coldest night of my life on the overnight train.

My visit coincided with a food and wine festival (fun) and a day sitting in the town's dry river bed watching a 'regatta' called Henley On Todd.

At the time I wasn't a rower, had only ever sat in pleasure craft and had no idea that the future path of my life would entail a lot of rowing. But hey, drinking cold lager and picking up a frame boat and running down a gravel river bed round an oil drum and back seemed like a fun way to spend the day. They even gave me a participant's certificate.

Returning to Henley on Todd on a dusty August day this year, I found the atmosphere and genuine Australian fun for life as evident as my memories. This time I was part of the VIP tent and although my rowing knowledge has expanded in the intervening years, this did not serve me any better when it came to successfully navigating the racing schedule.

From the high street parade down the Todd Mall, though the Arrente (Aboriginal Tribal) welcome and the fancy dress bring your own boat contest, the day was a rainbow display of Australian good humour. The events had somewhat expanded since my last attendance and so I was able to see pick-up-your-boat-and-run events such as the Maxi Yacht of 10 people, the Rowing Fours and the Kayak race before moving onto the surf-board-on-rails events including a surf rescue and 'Oxford tubs' events.

Inventiveness matters at this regatta and watching your fellow humans suffering or humiliating themselves is part of the ritual. I had never seen human hamster wheels before, a budgie smuggler sprint (look it up), nor sand shovelling, and my favourite, the water skis - four people using just one pair of skis.

My family were included in the event because it was the 150th anniversary of the completion of the "Overland Telegraph" line - the first electrical communication between Australia and the outside world. Morse code messages could now reach to the new colony from New York, London or Singapore in hours instead of letters sent by ship. My ancestor, Charles Todd, was in charge of the project and his wife, Alice, is memorialised in naming the oasis around which the town grew up.

On the day, I did manage to compete in the regatta and even met someone who is also a sculler - she spotted my carefully selected

115

kangaroo row suit and said "You're wearing a zootie", to which I replied, "You're a rower!"

I now claim the title of probably being the only person in the world to have attended both Henley and Henley on Todd in the same year... I just need Royal Canadian Henley to complete my hat trick of events.

Volker Nolte

Volker Nolte rowed for Germany and was an early tester of the sliding rigger single (published in Rowing Tales 2017). He has clearly enjoyed trying new equipment because he sent us this story about the development of oars after the Macon Oar.

Learning to Row with a New Type of Blade

In the fall of 1991, a group of Canadian lightweight rowers convinced me to conduct training camps with the goal of building a competitive big boat for the 1992 World Championships. We organized training weekends with the support of the rowers' clubs who provided rowing equipment and access to training water. The group grew nicely and in the spring of 1992, we were able to run competitive training sessions. Training and tests in small boats were very successful, and the skills of the rowers were polished rowing in big boats. It became clear that we would have enough top level athletes together to boat an eight with a solid chance to perform well on the international stage.

I brought my experience of coaching internationally-successful sculling boats to the whole project, and was also familiar with planning training and managing athletes of this caliber, but it was a new challenge for me to become proficient with teaching and correcting sweep rowing. I specifically focused on watching the blades to be able to identify the necessary stroke lengths and bladework for high level sweep boats.

Extensive usage of photos and videos helped me to improve these coaching skills and I became good at identifying the smallest differences in catch and finish timings. I became very confident in recognising which blade was even a small margin out of synch with the others.

As the interested reader will remember, at that time we used Macon Blades, and those were the blades I trained my eyes on. However, one day the newly developed Big Blades arrived in our camp when Concept2 provided some clubs with a set of the new oars to try them out. Because of the new asymmetric shape of the blades they were also called "Hatchet Oars", a name that described the newly developed shape quite accurately. Of course, no one had experience with these new blades. The only information provided was that the overall length of the delivered test oars – which were of fixed lengths (the adjustable length handles were not yet developed) - had to be shorter than those of our Macon oars. So, we set the inboards of the Big Blades to the exact length of our Macon oars, which made it easy to swap the two types of equipment from one training session to the next.

The rowers seemed to have fewer problems using the new blades than I had observing them operating the new equipment. Watching the Big Blades provided a completely different view – at least to me – so, I had to start over with training my eyes to be able to give accurate feedback. I felt that we had made good progress with the Macon oars and the new blades became for me more of an interruption than an addition to our training. It also was not directly obvious that the crews rowed faster with the new blades. Especially as the pairs lost a little of their balance and stability, since the outboard of the Big Blades were of course shorter and lighter than the old Macons.

Rowing the Big Blades in the eight also made the bladework initially a little messier especially at higher stroke rates, so that I became quite uncertain if the new equipment was an improvement to our program. Let's say this way: The new blades and I did not become immediate friends. However, the athletes' feedback was different. They mostly liked the sensation of the quicker lock-on with the Big Blades during the entry and the more solid feel of the pressure on the spoon during the drive. Needless to say, it became more and more a big question mark whether we should continue to use our old blades or if we should switch to the new ones.

To answer the question, we needed to do some testing to find convincing answers for the rowers and for me. But which test should we do? We had a vague idea how the Dreissigacker brothers (owners of Concept2 who designed the blades) compared the different blades, but we couldn't get our hands on their specific test data. At that time, we did not have access to any advanced biomechanics measurement equipment either.

So, we tried a few things.

Could you row higher stroke rates with one set of blades? No! Did it feel easier with the new blades to maintain a certain speed or stroke rate? No! How was the long distance training speed affected by the choice of blades? Not conclusive! Some crews rowed faster with the one set, some were faster with the other set, some did not see any changes. The start was faster with the Macon oars. 500m seemed to be a little faster with the new blades. Longer pieces were often affected by wind. All in all, it seemed difficult to find a proper way to accurately compare the two blade types. The differences we detected were too small to reliably make a decision.

Until I thought I had the best idea ever.

I explained it to the rowers and they were immediately agreeable to try this procedure.

So, here we go: Since our goal was to compete in the eight, this boat was chosen for the test. We put the Big Blades on port side and on starboard the Macon Blades. If one blade was superior to the other, the boat would turn to that side with the better blades showing their advantage – at least in theory. To make it objective, I even took the rudder off the boat, so that the coxswain could not influence the run of the boat. In addition, and for the same reason, the athletes had to row with their eyes closed so that they would not become biased in the process and they were instructed to row as consistently as possible with their best effort.

First, they had to row at their normal long distance training speed. Then we did pieces with increasing stroke rates and finally, we did a start. And all the time: The boat went straight! Then we switched the boat sides at which the different blades were used and, guess what, again the boat went dead straight.

With the measurement equipment we had and the circumstances we were in, we could not find strong enough evidence to choose one blade over the other. However, all the testing took some time and the athletes had a chance to get more used to the Big Blades. Their bladework improved and they developed more feel for the new blades. They stated that the new oars were easier to row, the blade was sitting better in the water and finally, they gained confidence that they could apply their power more directly especially when they were fatigued. So, it became clear that the athletes preferred the Big Blades over the older type of blades and they made the final decision.

We never looked back!

The 1992 Canadian lightweight men's eight won the US National Championships and came 4th at the World Championships setting a Canadian record that still stands today. Six of the rowers and the coxswain went on to row the next year at the World Championships winning the Gold Medal and beating the lightweight powerhouse countries Denmark, Italy, Great Britain and the USA using the new Hatchet Blades.

Sherri Cassuto

Sherri Cassuto represented the USA in the 1985 World Championships winning a silver in the pair, in 1987 in the single scull, and at the 1988 Olympics in the quad. She was taught to scull by Frank Cunningham at Lake Washington Rowing Club, Seattle, USA.

Professional watermen had an unique sculling technique called the 'waterman's catch' which was much admired and emulated in the mid 20th Century. I had never seen it demonstrated nor coached. Until, by good fortune, I found John Biglow's YouTube channel on which he interviewed Sherri demonstrating the technique in her single. She had been taught this way as a beginner and preferred to scull with a waterman's catch. This is how she described how to do it, the advantages of using it in racing starts and her lack of back injuries.

Sherri describes the US rowing style as 'early roll up' to contrast with the waterman 'flip' catch.

Watch the video https://www.youtube.com/watch?v=vXHYPUY2QqI

Thames Watermans Style

The Watermans Catch

As long as the end of the oar touches the water the water catches it itself.

I'm Sherri Cassuto and I had the privilege of being coached by Frank Cunningham when I first learned how to row. I moved to Seattle in 1978 and I had never rowed before. And I was entranced with singles when I saw them at the Kings Point Boathouse when I was there to sail.

And just say that I was very resourceful. I didn't know singles existed. I found out that Lake Washington Rowing Club existed, they had no telephone or anything. And I showed up all the time until I finally could join and started out learning in a wherry. Frank was the coach there and that's how I first started rowing.

After I started racing, I realized I was doing pretty well and I had the additional privilege of being near the University of Washington and having the national team coach Bob Ernst over there at the Conibear Boathouse, so I got to train with him and all the scullers and sweep rowers he was training so I got great training over there.

Because Frank was really passionate about the Thames Waterman style. He taught it to me as well as the handful of other people. He really gave me no option but to choose it because he proved to me again and again on the water that it was the better choice. And when I was a good enough sculler to prove that to myself on the water I would row alternating between the two different styles and I'm convinced that it's a faster rowing style, even though it remains unpopular.

I tested the two styles to see which was faster while doing 500 m pieces. I would do six in a workout. And I would take into account the speed of the water through the [Montlake] Cut and I would do the first piece the Thames Waterman style, the second piece USRA style, third piece Thames style, and compare the times. The next workout I did the US style first and then the Thames style second and alternated that way. I was a scientist and I needed to prove it to myself, which was faster? Because I wouldn't commit unless it was faster because it was too big a risk. But it was faster.

Maybe because it's an old style, the Thames Waterman style. It's really fallen out of favor. And there's a tremendous amount of resistance on the upper levels of Rowing to rowing this way. The people who really learned from the old Thames Watermen are gone now. This style has a risk of being lost and so I am thrilled to get the chance to row what I know of it and record it so that it stays around.

As I became known as a sculler I tried out for the US sculling team using this style and it was very unpopular in the USRA and the coaches argued with me about it a lot. They thought I should just stop using it. I should get with the program and start using the USRA style.

But you know when you're trying to be the fastest you could possibly be and you've just proven to yourself that what you're using is faster, you can't go backwards.

So the hallmark of this was me going out to the US singles trials and I was doing my very ritualized warmup and as I was getting my oars out on the dock one of the national team coaches came alongside me and started arguing with me about my rowing style. And said that I couldn't do that. I just couldn't row that way that I was out of my mind for doing that. And I looked at them and I said look, if I'm rowing in my boat I'll row my way, if I'm rowing in your boat I'll row your way, I've got to warm up, can we not talk about this now?

So it was a problem. They really didn't like it.

But fortunately I had had enough training in the USRA style that if I was rowing in a team boat, I could adapt because like I said before, the most important thing is that you're doing the same thing in the boat as everyone else.

Frank was saying, especially that if I was gonna row this way, that I could start faster than if you have to start with your blade squared. At the start, it's very hard to time the legs and get a really solid drive on the first stroke. Because it's precarious. You're perched in an odd position. So what he had me do (in those days they started races by saying "Etes-vous prêts? Partez"). So he had me sit about three quarters slide with my blades comfortably flat on the water. Remember you can move in the boat before the start as long as the boat itself does not move before the start is called.

When they said "Etes-vous prêts?" I would squeeze the blades out and square so that when Partez happened my catch would be like this. [She demonstrates a quick square and first stroke.] The blades would just bury themselves to the proper depth. And you could drive with all the force you wanted in your life and get a really good super stroke. He had the second stroke be really, really short so that you keep your momentum going for the second stroke.

When I started sweep rowing the style was the East German C-back position. And everyone was approximating rowing like that and as you know the most important thing in rowing is that everybody does the same thing. But people were getting hurt. There were a lot of back injuries.

Most people don't know this but at the very first women's national Powerlifting Championships I got second. So I have a lot of experience of weightlifting. And I think that the important lesson that we can learn about rowing style comes from weightlifters. One of the hallmarks of the old Thames Waterman style is that the finish is squeezed through with the shoulders, chest up, squeezed through with the shoulders and you finish tall and then immediately snap your pelvis behind you with your hands out quickly so it's finished like this. And you snap yourself out of the bow so that the bow doesn't plow down. It stays high. And you get yourself out to half slide and then slowly continue the rest of the slide to the catch and it's much stronger and much safer.

I don't know anybody who rows this way that got a back injury from rowing. And I've had this discussion with people time and time again, to be relaxed and in a neutral spine position but for us we sit so much nowadays that neutral ends up not being neutral. It's like a slouch.

You'll never ever see a weightlifter deadlifting in a slouch, they hurt themselves. They all very studiously stick their pelvis out behind them. Chest up look at a point high up off the wall and deadlift from this position, because they know that it's strongest and safest. And they're the ones that have to use the strongest position available because it's all about how much weight they can lift. So I think we can take the lesson from the discipline of weightlifting, that there really is no question, that this is not only a safer body position but far stronger.

How's your health these days? [the video is dated 14th October, 2015]

I have stage four colon cancer. I was diagnosed with it in the first week of January 2014. And I was given six months to two years to live and it's almost two years now. So considering my health on paper, my health is terrible. But I feel really good. And in part I feel really good because of a life of exercise and the priority of a life of exercise.

[Sherri Cassuto died 29th April, 2016.]

Trevor Shiels

Trevor Shiels is from New South Wales, Australia. He echoes many other rowers with this story about personal motivation and the rewards of completing a workout.

Erg Love Hate

Woke up and it's raining again today, I thought about the erg. I haven't been on it since the last rain set in. I made a coffee, sat on the lounge and thought again of the erg. I became nervous and tried to delay it. I walked reluctantly down the stairs and laid the erg down. I was anxious, like standing on the bank waiting to push off before a race.

Thoughts of those killer sessions and starving for breath raced through my head.

I put my shoes on and settled in, pushing the first couple of strokes felt like I had the choke on. The muscles fighting against it.

Worked through the session and stepped off it like a new man.

Traumatic yet rewarding.

I have a love-hate relationship with the erg.

Charles Wemyss

Charles Wemyss (who wrote another tale in this volume) also shared this lovely manta from his time coaching at Berwick Academy School in Maine, USA.

The Rowing Mantra

At Berwick we had a little mantra that we used most days after practice.

"What do we do?" "We row."

"Why do we row?" "For body, soul and spirit!"

"How do we row?" "With technical excellence and strength!"

"Who are we?" "We are Berwick Crew."

It is all really that simple.